SHE MUST HAVE BEEN A BEAUTIFUL BABY— BECAUSE, BABY, LOOK AT HER NOW!

From childhood to superstardom,
Farrah Fawcett-Majors is an
American success story:

As an adored child growing up in Texas . . .
as a beauty contest-winning college coed
starring both in the classroom and on the
tennis courts . . . as a performer in
TV commercials that within two years made
her face and figure famous from coast to coast
. . . and as a knockout hit in her first
major TV role.

Farrah has always been what every woman
dreams of being and every man dreams
of having.

It's all beautifully spelled out in—

FARRAH

FARRAH

An Unauthorized Biography of Farrah Fawcett-Majors

by
Patricia Burstein

A SIGNET BOOK
NEW AMERICAN LIBRARY
TIMES MIRROR

NAL BOOKS ARE ALSO AVAILABLE AT DISCOUNTS
IN BULK QUANTITY FOR INDUSTRIAL OR
SALES-PROMOTIONAL USE. FOR DETAILS, WRITE TO
PREMIUM MARKETING DIVISION,
NEW AMERICAN LIBRARY, INC., 1301 AVENUE OF THE AMERICAS,
NEW YORK, NEW YORK 10019.

SIGNET TRADEMARK REG. U.S. PAT. OFF. AND FOREIGN COUNTRIES
REGISTERED TRADEMARK— MARCA REGISTRADA
HECHO EN CHICAGO, U.S.A.

SIGNET, SIGNET CLASSICS, MENTOR, PLUME AND
MERIDIAN BOOKS
are published by The New American Library, Inc.,
1301 Avenue of the Americas, New York, New York 10019.

First Signet Printing, June, 1977

1 2 3 4 5 6 7 8 9

PRINTED IN THE UNITED STATES OF AMERICA

To my parents, three sisters
(Jessica, Ellen and Karen), two brothers
(John and Judd), and Cloud.

Personal thanks to Patrick and Peggy Dunne
and Veronica Hirsch who put me up—
and also put up with me—on this project.
Professional gratitude to *People*
Managing Editor Richard B. Stolley and
Senior Editor William F. Ewald,
for allowing me every possible opportunity
to learn and grow in my work.
And thanks, of course, to Freya Manston,
my indefatigable agent.

Contents

Prologue: The Farrah Phenomenon   1

Chapter 1: A Child in Corpus Christi   5

Chapter 2: Campus Beauty Queen   17

Chapter 3: Farrah Heads for Hollywood   33

Chapter 4: Marriage for a One-Man Woman   50

Chapter 5: Hair—and Other Beauty Hints   65

Chapter 6: Charlie's Angels   80

Chapter 7: Farrah at Play   100

Chapter 8: Farrah's Philosophy   113

Chapter 9: Farrah's Future   127

Chapter 10: Farrah-Fitness   151

☆

FARRAH

Prologue:

The Farrah Phenomenon

Just as the bare crescent of dawn makes its debut over the Hollywood Hills, a silken hand gropes for the alarm clock. One of the world's most beautiful women gets out of bed. She tiptoes around the room so as not to awaken her husband. After showering and washing her hair she slips into a pair of snug blue jeans. Depending on the day, she may straighten up a room or plan a menu. But she always scribbles an affectionate note to her spouse whose day starts an hour-and-a-half later at 6:30 A.M. Outside, a limousine purrs in the huge circular driveway of her Bel Air mansion. She sleepwalks out the French Provincial door and into the damp darkness. Thirteen hours later she will be delivered back to this doorstep, in time to jump into the shower, mist herself with perfume, and become the Total Woman once again.

Farrah Fawcett-Majors, America's fantasy, has the schedule of a long-distance trucker. And it is by choice. Hers is the face that launched a hundred products (Noxzema, Ultra-Brite, Mercury-Cougar), but she is not content to luxuriate behind that luscious beauty. Farrah, the breath-stopping superstar of "Charlie's Angels," has tumbling blond hair, show-white teeth, emerald eyes, and a sleek 5-foot 6-inch, 112-pound frame. She also comes in doll size, T-shirts, and posters, all record-smashing. Farrah earns a six-figure salary and has a Six-Million-Dollar Man, actor Lee Majors, for a husband.

Still, Charlie's sexiest Angel has a headier mission than donning a bikini to cover up the show's sometimes skimpy dialogue. The Woman-with-Everything also happens to have a dream. To be a fine actress. Already lionized by the public as the Pinup Girl of the 70s, Farrah squealed with pleasure recently about signing "actress" instead of "model" on a form for her doctor. The well-brought-up daughter of a Texas businessman frets: "It's the old Marilyn Monroe syndrome. Nobody takes a pretty girl seriously."

But as it turns out, *nobody* takes offense at this gorgeous sex symbol. While Farrah trades openly on her beauty—and why not—she is enormously comfortable with it. She even displays a sense of humor about her great looks by flashing her Carter-like choppers. "It was touch-and-go at first," flawless Farrah cracks after a makeup session on the "Charlie" set. But more than this, Farrah has a wholesome, honest quality that disarms a potentially jealous audience hopelessly aspiring to look like her. After all, who could say sinful things

2

about a Hollywood star who faithfully counts rosary beads at bedtime? And whose contract has a clause that she must be off the set by 7:00 P.M. to dine with her husband?

Farrah Fawcett-Majors is truly a phenomenon. Teenagers poster their bedroom walls with her picture. Adult admirers unabashedly decorate offices in the same fashion. Anybody who takes care of a home cheers Farrah for her spic-and-span appearance. Even television critics, hardly bowled over by "Charlie's Angels," are dazzled by Farrah. Says Chicago *Daily News* TV critic Frank Swertlow: "Farrah is a human meringue, the eternal snowflake who will always dance above the earth. She is a fantasy in an age that doesn't want reality." Everybody is enchanted with her!

Farrah has risen to success like a comely comet. She is the first actress known to emerge as a major star on the basis of thirty-second spots and a poster. The incredible Angel, as agile on the athletic field as on the dance floor, has set new and different records in just six years. Farrah-gilded covers of such national magazines as *Time* and *TV Guide* became the year's bestsellers. She landed on the cover of *People* three times with the two other Angels, then with husband Lee Majors, and finally as the lead cover picture of the Year-End issue. Predictably, she turned up as a weekly fixture in the tabloids and fan magazines. A *Scholastic Magazine* poll of 14,000 junior and senior high school students nationwide found Farrah to be their "personal hero." (She coasted into first place with 2,001 votes, as compared with comedian Jerry Lewis, second with a mere 828 votes.) To cheer up listeners last winter, Detroit deejay Dick Purtan ran a

Farrah Fawcett-Majors look-alike contest. Instantly 380 would-be FF-Ms fluffed up their hair and signed on. Farrah even ended up as a Back-of-the-Book cultural curiosity in the intellectually elitist *New Republic*, with a headline "Don't Change a Hair for Me."

With characteristic modesty, unflappable Farrah Fawcett-Majors says, "I never felt I needed to be a star. I always got along in life just fine."

Chapter 1

A Child in Corpus Christi

On February 2, 1947, at exactly 3:10 P. M. Farrah Leni Fawcett entered the world in the palm-fringed south Texas coastal city of Corpus Christi. She was the second child born to James William Fawcett, a twenty-nine-year-old pipefitter for an oil refinery, and his wife, Pauline Alice Evans, who at thirty-two was three years his senior. Nine years earlier they had their first child, a daughter they named Dianne.

Farrah seemed to get off to an inauspicious start. First of all, to make a February debut seemed as ominous as what natives call the "blue norther" that mercilessly whips the normally subtropical area; February is the cruelest month of the year in Corpus Christi. Then, Farrah's name was mis-spelled—Ferrah—on her birth certificate. And in class-conscious Corpus Christi, dominated by blueblood Irish and Czechoslovakian immigrant farmers and flavored by a substantial Mexican population, Farrah was born in a hospital on the wrong side of town. Memorial Hospital, then a grouping of manila modules on a parched patch of lawn, was in sharp contrast to Spohn, a private Catholic hospital hovering over the horseshoe-shaped bay, framed by lush banana trees and staffed with nuns in crisp white uniforms. Memorial was the county hospital, and it was to Memorial that the one-month-old baby Farrah returned so doctors could repair a twisted intestine.

Nonetheless, Farrah, equipped with an Aquarian optimism, weathered the potential storm. Bolstered by her father who came from the north Texas farm community of Hillsboro, and by her mother who was reared in Henrietta, Oklahoma, she developed self-confidence and pride that allowed her to feel comfortable anywhere. She also inherited golden good looks from a father whom friends describe as astonishingly handsome, and a sunny disposition from a mother who set an example by always taking care of herself. Both parents instilled their children with a sense of direction and an ambition to succeed. By the time Farrah was fifteen, her father had traded in the khaki work clothes he wore while supervising a crew of pipefitters for a business suit as founder and head of a pipeline construction company. Today he runs a custodial service for suburban banks in Houston, where the Fawcetts moved when Farrah went off to college. As the family fortunes improved, the Fawcetts moved four times in Corpus Christi. Farrah's first home was garage-sized and a block away from a low-income housing project. By the time she reached high school, the Fawcetts were comfortably installed in a white brick split-level with an ample lawn graced by gas lamps, spruce palms, a date palm, and neatly trimmed hedges. The house was a mere five blocks from posh Ocean Drive with its sumptuous mansions.

From infancy Farrah became the object of a doting public that consisted of her parents, a protective older sister, and assorted relatives and neighbors. Mrs. Eddie Lee Winkelmann, who at one time lived directly across the street from the Fawcetts, remembers Farrah as a two-year-old: "She was a beautiful bronzed baby and her little curls were platinum." Dianne Fawcett often looked after her little sister when their mother suffered from the migraine headaches that sent her to bed for days at a stretch. The only two-year-old girl on the block, Farrah usually tagged along with children a year or two older. She would sit in a wagon pulled by them. But her favorite place was a swing in her own backyard, and there was no limit to how high she would soar on it. Her decisiveness was evident even at that early age: she stayed away from the seesaw. She displayed an intelligence beyond her years. "Farrah was a good little talker," recalls Mrs. Winkelmann, whose miniature black collie got its feet caught between the slats of lawn furniture. The puppy's yelps for help were answered by Farrah, who, though panic-stricken like the other children, instantly set a rescue mission in action by informing Mrs. Winkelmann of the mishap. Farrah also showed a dislike of monsters early on. Mrs. Winkelmann remembers a movie outing when Farrah sat on her lap and announced midway through the film, "I don't like that boy." The movie was *Frankenstein*.

Her parents enrolled Farrah in St. Patrick's School, a Catholic institution largely attended by the upper crust of Corpus Christi. They plunked down $20 a month for a strong educationaˡ program coupled with a daily regimen of religion. Outside the white Mediterranean-style school building, shaped like a tuning fork, Farrah lined up with classmates in columns of two for the march across the driveway to daily Mass followed by catechism as the first class of the day. In their uniforms—the girls in green skirts and white blouses and the boys in khaki pants and white T-shirts with a green emblem—they looked like a legion of leprechauns. Farrah wore a green beanie, emblazoned with the school initials in felt, and she kept rosary beads in her pockets. Once inside the church, nuns patrolled the aisles with rulers to keep students from slumping in their seats or resting elbows on the pews. The future Angel was required to recite faultlessly such heavenly lines as "Hail Mary, full of grace, the Lord is with thee, blessed art Thou amongst women . . ." Apparently the words lodged permanently in Farrah's psyche. "I believe that if a person is born and she is exceptionally *blessed*," Farrah has repeatedly told interviewers, "then she has at one time or another paid her dues." If the litany did not purge students of impure thoughts, a parental social code, setting 9:00 P.M. party curfews for seventh-graders, did the trick.

Farrah was baptized at age two at Christ the King Church, easily recognizable by its purple-tile and brick exterior and a picture window featuring a large statue of Christ the King with a crown on his head. Normally, baptism is performed within a month after birth, but Farrah was a convert to Catholicism. Her sister, baptized the same day, was ten years old at the time. Their saints' names, required for baptism, were Mary Farrah Leni Fawcett and Theresa Dianne Fawcett. In 1954, the year her father was baptized, Farrah, then seven, received communion and was confirmed. Friends do not know whether Mrs. Fawcett went through the rite, but report that the Fawcetts, not unlike most converts, were fiercely religious. Mrs. Louise Smejkal, a close neighbor, recalls how the Fawcetts, particularly Farrah and Dianne, liked to accompany her family to church. After a short while, it became a habit, and the Fawcetts decided to sign on as bona-fide church members. "Farrah was one of the flower girls at my older daughter's wedding," Mrs. Smejkal says. "She was so beautiful. She looked just like a little angel."

Sisters at St. Patrick's remember that there was a special glow about Farrah. Her academic record was also unblemished. Sister Aloysius Young, who taught Farrah in the third grade, says she was a straight-A student. "She was a precious little girl," the sister proudly states. "She always cooperated with a smile on her face." In a scrapbook Sister Aloysius keeps on each of her present and past students there is a school picture of Farrah with a beanie atop her celestial curls as well as a newspaper photo taken of Farrah as a college beauty queen. Sister Aloysius also saved one of Farrah's compositions: "I would like to be a Sister when I grow up." Other girls expressed the same desire. "Sometimes it turns out, sometimes not," she comments wryly.

Nevertheless, Farrah continued to show unflinching devotion to her school duties. Seventh-grade teacher Sister Damien Ordener describes Farrah then as "pure as crystal with nothing to hide." When some of the students engraved their initials on the old-fashioned slant-top desks, Sister Damien made everyone stay after school to sand the tops. Farrah, whom she never considered a culprit, quietly shared the punishment: "Farrah was happy-go-lucky. Like Humpty-Dumpty she could overcome anything. If anything got her down, she was instantly up on her feet again."

Outside of school Farrah earned the same respect from neighbors. In her pre-teen years she began to babysit for them. Farrah, now asking $10,000 a show for "Charlie" collected fifty cents an hour in those days. One client was neighbor Mrs. Jesse Ocker who had two sons, eight and two at the time. The younger boy had a hearing disability, and this made Mrs. Ocker especially cautious about babysitters. She favored Farrah above all others. "I wouldn't leave my boy with just anybody," Mrs. Ocker explains. "Farrah was somebody very special. She was reliable and responsible. Some young people don't have the time to talk to older people, but Farrah always had the time to speak." Around her junior year in high school Farrah began gradually to phase out of the babysitting business.

High school was a busy time for Farrah. There were her studies, football games, friends and dates, not necessarily in descending order of importance. During those years students preferred malted milks to marijuana, and slumber parties were held at friends' homes instead of the principal's office. At the W. B. Ray High School, within walking distance of Farrah's home, a motel-like marquee on the front lawn advertises football games. Students successfully petitioned authorities to change the name of the street fronting the school from Minnesota to Texan Trail, in honor of their team, the Fighting Texans.

Farrah's popularity did not intrude on her above-average grades. Dubbed "Most Beautiful" girl in her class throughout high school, Farrah paid more attention to her homework than the mirror. Annette Grossman Klein, the girl who was voted "Most Likely to Succeed" in their senior year, is today married to a lawyer and raising a four-month-old baby. The daughter of a prominent Corpus Christi dermatologist, she taught children with learning disabilities before devoting full time to her family. Of Farrah Fawcett, she says, "Now that I think of it, Farrah was always striving. She always had something to do—exercising while other kids were eating hamburgers." Another classmate, whose younger brother is smitten with the superstar, remembers Farrah coming over to her house for help with an algebra problem just prior to a test: "I couldn't believe it, because Farrah was so intelligent." Another former classmate, who was a top-notch student, calls Farrah generous for golfing with her: "I was a A-plus student and not all that popular. And here this beautiful, adored girl was being so nice to me. I really appreciated it. She was a great golfer, a tremendous athlete. She is not a dumb blonde by any means!"

Her academic record reflected that opinion. History teacher Dan Purcell gave Farrah an "A" in his class and remembers her doing just as well in other courses. "She was a real clean-cut, wholesome young lady, and she was very punctual." In those days, Purcell adds, there were no "girls' sports" and thus Farrah did not get an opportunity to lead a team to victory. But her talent was visible in another area. Observes renowned Texas artist Joseph Cain, today head of the art department at a local college: "She caught on quickly to concepts and had an understanding beyond that of other students. Farrah showed particular ability with 3-D forms in clay and plaster carving. She also did watercolors and was particularly good with human figures, whether painting or sculpting them." He also spotted her beauty—"changeable eyes flashing and quiet, but with an almost feline glow," and asked her to pose for an evening Life Drawing class. "An indication of her shyness," Cain points out, "is that when I told her that most of the models posed in bathing suits Farrah refused to do this. She wore a dress." Then he adds: "She was sort of a contradiction. She was quiet and reserved in class, but her eyes sparkled with ideas. Everyone thought she was beautiful so Farrah sort of withdrew to keep from posing. I'll say one thing though—her presence kept the class awake after lunch."

Though Farrah did not take part in extracurricular activities—not even the National Thespian Society, Bible Club, or Future Homemakers—everybody knew her. The name, Farrah Fawcett, aroused a certain fascination. But like everything about Farrah, then and now, it was no mere Hollywood invention. It had come to her mother in a flash. Farrah sounded good with Fawcett, and that was that. Clearly Farrah Fawcett was much more than a name. She was the apotheosis of the American Dream, beautiful, bright, athletic, wholesome, appealing as apple pie à la mode. "She never went through an awkward period," says Donna Alexander Schenker, a three-time runner-up for "Most Beautiful" and now married to an attorney and working as a librarian in a San Antonio elementary school. "Farrah never lorded it over anybody. When I lost to her at the 'Favorites' dance where they decide the contest, Farrah just acted like her title wasn't important." Donna, whose debutante party was the highlight of the year, counted Farrah as a close friend: "There were about eight of us who ran around together at parties, football games, slumber parties, and just driving around in cars." They were also bunkmates the summer of 1962 at Camp Arrowhead in Kerville, Texas. "Everybody loved Farrah," Donna recalls. "She was a tremendous swimmer and tennis player. She had the lead in a camp play too. Farrah was always a knock-out."

Gary Roberts, today a thirty-two-year-old real estate broker in Corpus Christi, was among the Farrah-struck boys at W. B. Ray High School. He had noticed Farrah but hesitated to ask her out because she was younger. He was only two years older, but the age gap seemed too wide then. "It was sort of like your friend's little sister growing up," he explains. When Farrah reached ninth grade, his self-imposed probation was up, and he finally asked her for a date after a few parties they attended with other friends. "When you're bitten, snowed, in high school with your first love," Gary says, "it is an important part of your life always. I still consider her a friend." Farrah, a one-man woman from the start, felt the same way. The two were like Siamese twins, talking on the phone at least twice each weekday night and going on weekends to movies, football games, and the annual Ritter dance, a gala cowboy-style event held at Exposition Hall. Every morning Gary picked Farrah up in a blue Chevrolet and deposited her back on her doorstep at the end of the school day. As presents, he gave her charms for her bracelet.

Gary remembers her parents as "super nice" and says they always made him feel right at home. "They trusted Farrah," he says. "Her mother would ask 'What are you kids going to do tonight?' so she was always conscious of where Farrah was, and didn't worry." They always heeded the curfew. Occasionally they would go on weekends to his parents' ranch where Farrah liked to ride horses. Usually they went with a group of friends. After Gary and the other boys shot quail and duck, Farrah and her female companions would retrieve the birds. Small wonder that Farrah currently boasts about how husband Lee Majors lets her do the shooting.

Gary, who played football his freshman year and then decided to become a rodeo athlete in his free time, liked to wear Levi's and boots. "I went South Texas western style," he says. "Farrah wore mostly dresses. She always looked really nice. She was weight-conscious and aware of how she looked."

Even as a teenager, friends say, Farrah had a flair for fashion. Mrs. Estelle Ross, a family friend and dressmaker, created part of Farrah's wardrobe: "Her favorite colors were blue and green." Among the outfits she made for Farrah were a long pink glazed cotton flowered dress with a high waistline, and a knee-length A-line, V-necked white pique dress with a frilly bodice. Both were for parties and teas. "Farrah was always so sweet and appreciative," says Mrs. Ross, who also designed clothes for sister Dianne, who was "a different type than Farrah, not as outgoing and a little more nervous." After high school they lost touch, but Farrah remembered Mrs. Ross when it came time to mail out wedding invitations. "I couldn't go," Mrs. Ross sighs, "but I treasure that invitation."

Marriage to Farrah crossed Gary Roberts' mind, but in his sophomore year of college he chose another woman. His first year away, Farrah reserved weekends, Christmas and Easter and other holidays for him. But her mother encouraged her to keep busy and go out with others. "We stopped dating on an amiable basis," says Roberts, whose wife met and liked Farrah. "We go out of our way to look and see how she's doing."

His replacement was football player Mike Blaine, and again Farrah was unwavering in the attention she lavished on him. They saw each other constantly during Farrah's junior and senior years, and he gave her his football jacket. Then Farrah did the leave-taking, going off to college in Austin. Blaine, a year younger, admired her athleticism. They went horseback riding and made trips to the beach, where gathering sand dollars is a favorite local pastime. "She was a real nice girl," Mike, now married and working in construction, says enthusiastically.

Both men, constantly badgered by reporters, try to protect Farrah's privacy. "I made an attempt to call her," says the long-lashed, blue-eyed Roberts. "I wanted to know what we could say in the interest of her career. So many people have jumped on the bandwagon for attention. Mike and I are the only two who dated her. I know that one day our paths will cross, and I would hate to think of Farrah saying, 'Hey, you're the guy who said ...' meaning something a stranger told the press." Roberts, unable to get through press agents, left a message for her. He has not heard from her yet, though he occasionally chats with her father when he comes to Corpus Christi on business.

For a long time to come, Farrah will continue to be heard from across the land. This Corpus Christi honor student and all-American beauty, who came into the world in a tornado-threatened season, has hit the country like a huge hurricane. "There were many beautiful girls in her class," artist Joseph Cain comments, "but Farrah had the most striking effect." A newspaper cover photo of Farrah adorns the high school bulletin board. A strip of paper, tacked under it, reads "Class of 1965." She remains the talk of the town called Corpus Christi, and all of it is flattering. Locals remember her fondly. And Farrah Fawcett has never forgotten them. Fortified with love and devotion acquired in her hometown, Farrah has her roots here.

Just as sure as the bluebonnets bloom in Corpus Christi, Farrah was certain she would return one day. That thought was on her mind as she packed to go off to college. Wherever Farrah Fawcett's future would lead, Corpus Christi would stay in her suitcase and her soul.

Chapter 2

Campus Beauty Queen

When Farrah headed for the University of Texas at Austin the next fall, her mother told her, "I don't expect you to be on the honor roll up there, but I want you to have good time." Such advice was consistent with Mrs. Fawcett's philosophy. She was all for Farrah having fun, as long as it did not hurt anyone. On at least one occasion, friends remember her chaperoning them on a childhood escapade. A favorite prank was rolling toilet tissue over someone's house. Known as Texas-style graffiti, this was accomplished by throwing the tissue paper high into the trees and then dragging it all over the property. Karen Spellings, a college friend who grew up with Farrah in Corpus Christi, remembers that Farrah's mother drove them to the house: "When you think of it, this was a lot safer than her not knowing where Farrah was. Mrs.

Fawcett was always interested in everything Farrah was doing, and she also showed concern for her daughter's friends. We used to love to go over to Farrah's house and sit around talking with her mother." The feeling was apparently mutual because today these same friends refer affectionately to her by her nickname, "Polly."

From the moment Farrah arrived at the university she heeded her mother's words. As it happened, she had no choice. Sorority rush, a rite of passage in Texas society, was already in full swing her first day there. It was a week of nonstop parties. But for some girls it spelled a tense time. Under a scorching September sun, they had to devise ways to get from the dormitories to the sorority houses without a hair falling out of place on their heads. Socially astute and monied mothers from Houston and Dallas would suffer a few days in an inelegant motel nearby so that their daughters could drive the family car and arrive unruffled in their *de rigueur* dark cotton dresses. Freshmen were not allowed to have cars on campus, but as sophomores the next year they would surely show up in late-model convertibles and sports cars. "Farrah and the rest of us walked and sweated," recalls Arden Westbrook, a college and later California roommate. "On pledge night we were all standing in line and the fraternities came over and all these guys just bunched up around Farrah. There must have been five hundred guys standing around her."

Farrah pledged Delta Delta Delta, known as Tri-Delt, and ranked fourth in the Hellenic hierarchy. The top three sororities—Pi Beta Phi, Kappa Kappa Gamma, and Kappa Alpha Theta—only wanted genetic miracles such as girls born into old establishment families. Even Tracy Connally, daughter-in-law of former Texas governor John Connally, was a Tri-Delt. No matter that her father-in-law was a prominent Houston attorney, Secretary of the Navy, and would later be appointed Treasury Secretary. Like Farrah's father, his beginnings had been blue-collar as a bus driver in the backwaters of Texas.

Tri-Delt attracted a collection of golden beauties. Farrah was the fairest of them all with her perfect hair and perfect figure. "Farrah was the most beautiful girl I had ever seen," one sorority sister remembers. "When I saw her the first time I thought to myself, 'This is too much competition!' But Farrah was so sweet that you couldn't be mad at her."

Some sorority sisters were not nearly as generous about Farrah's fantastic looks. In fact, her beauty and the resulting instant popularity created considerable jealousy. "Some of the girls were resentful because she was so cute and pretty," one Tri-Delt maintains. "The hair, the teeth, the incredible body. She was just so gorgeous." Sometimes the gossip was vicious. A few sorority sisters made up stories about Farrah having a bad reputation, and at least one or two stooped to saying she came from a "white trash" background. "Farrah was so decent and sweet," another sorority sister explains, "that the only thing they could come up with was the fact that she wasn't filthy rich or from a mainline Texas family." Nonetheless, Farrah, voted one of the Ten Most Beautiful Women, a rare honor for a freshman, knew enough to confine her beauty competitions to the state. "Farrah would never have entered the Miss America pageant," an Austin writer and observer of local sociological customs says. "That was for high school twirlers from some small town."

Farrah never took sorority life too seriously. "Oh, it was ridiculous," she told the Dallas *Times Herald* in a recent interview. "You were supposed to take this little book with you on pledge night and make dates. I had so many dates—I was booked up until February or something." Always something of a nonconformist, she seemed automatically to stand out from the crowd. While other girls were decked out in dresses, pantyhose, and Pappagallos, Farrah (who had changed her style somewhat from Corpus Christi days) wore jeans, sweaters, and her hair in bunches. In what became her trademark—white jeans, a blue workshirt, and Bernardo sandals—Farrah embodied the *au naturel* look long before her classmates knew such a thing existed. But in no time, the Farrah Fawcett style caught on and became the rage of the campus. It was always that way. By the end of rush week everybody at the University of Texas knew who Farrah Fawcett was, no small feat considering that the Brobdingnagian-sized school had about 26,000 students at the time.

During her freshman year Farrah majored in microbiology and thus did not earn high enough grades to be initiated into the sorority. This meant that Farrah, who remained a pledge, could not live at the Tri-Delt house. It was just as well because Farrah and the friends she met the first week and still keeps in contact with today were happily situated in Mayfair House, a huge cinderblock dormitory about ten blocks away from the campus. Some of them made the grades to move to the sorority house but preferred to remain at Mayfair. "Farrah was disappointed about the sorority thing only because she likes to succeed," one roommate explains. "But she has always had this marvelous attitude about going on to the next thing."

Clearly Farrah was not dependent on the sorority for an active social life. In one day she had more dates than other girls might have in a month. A slightly amused Susan Parker, another close roommate who also went with Farrah to California before returning to Texas to marry her high school sweetheart, comments: "A typical day in the life of Farrah Fawcett? Well, she had a date for breakfast and then she went to classes and after she had a lunch date and then she went to classes and afterwards she had a date before dinner and another date after dinner." Put another way by still another roommate: "Some of the guys just wouldn't leave Farrah alone. It was like a notch on their gun if they could take her to breakfast. With the majority of them she only went out once. But Farrah was always kind and polite to all of them."

By her sophomore year Farrah resumed her pattern as a one-man woman. She preferred this to a whirlwind of assorted dates. The man in her life for as long as she was to remain at the University of Texas was handsome Greg Lott, who was there on a football scholarship. Lott's sister, Shanny, a beautiful blonde, became one of Farrah's closest friends, and they still talk fairly regularly by phone. Shanny, now divorced, also married a football player, Texas quarterback James Street. "Farrah and my brother Greg were the dream couple at Texas," Shanny says wistfully. "In the end, Greg did not feel that he could set Farrah up in the style to which she was accustomed." Greg Lott was once pinned to Farrah, and today at thirty-one, a year older than Farrah, he remains unmarried and working for an oil company leasing mineral rights.

That same year Farrah switched her major to art and distinguished herself in this area. "She was my favorite student," Charles Umlauf, a prominent Texas sculptor whose "Spirit of Flight" sits at the entrance to the Dallas Love Field, exults. "I never had such a good student—neither before nor since Farrah." He also admired her beauty. And some students say that Umlauf was in love with her. He blushes at the suggestion, but does not deny it. "Farrah was such a natural beauty," he gushes. "She doesn't wear paint or anything. She always looked fresh as a daisy. She never smoked or drank, and I never heard a cuss word from her mouth. Farrah has a sculptured look, always changing with her moods. She will be around for a long time. Farrah is no flash-in-the-pan beauty."

Farrah was extremely attentive to his instruction and received top grades in his classes. "When I would be criticizing her," Umlauf recalls, "she would have her head right over my shoulder so she could hear every word. When I would ask why she was taking notes, she would say, 'I want to do it just like you!' She was driven, but not to the point of being strained. She just wanted to do her best." Farrah did charcoal and pen-and-ink drawings that were quite good, but she excelled most at sculpture. She also doubled as a model, and today a bust of her decorates Umlauf's sculptural garden in Austin. Farrah in clay is seated on a heart-shaped sculptured chair. Umlauf's studio along with his house is on the grounds, and it is here that Farrah worked for a day or two at a time en route to visiting her parents in Houston. "We would work all day," he says, "and break for meals my wife would prepare."

The respect was mutual. A bronze casting of one of Umlauf's most profound sculptures, "War Mother," sits in the living room of Farrah's Bel Air mansion. "You would think that a woman as pretty as Farrah would veer away from expressive works," Umlauf comments. "But she liked the idea of seeing honest expression in art such as suffering or poverty. She was attracted to the work of Goya and Modigliani. Farrah was an excellent student of art history."

Recently Farrah wrote to him on FF-M white embossed stationery: "I would love to have one of everything ... maybe that's why I am working so hard." Umlauf had sent Farrah a photograph of another sculpture he was doing of her, and she thanked him. "You really captured all the things I see in myself," she commented modestly. "In other words it's me, but better that I am!" The ever-religious Farrah also inquired about buying some "terra-cotta torsos or maybe a head of Pope John XXIII."

Since Farrah spent so much time in the art building, it was fortuitous that she was given a car her sophomore year. Her classroom was clear across campus. "Farrah was always lugging big sketch pads," a roommate recalls, "and she really needed a car to get to class." The car was a burgundy Riviera, a recent model but used. Her father had gotten a good bargain on it from a friend. It also proved to be a great deal for Farrah and her friends, who remember going everywhere in the car. "If one of

23

us wanted ice cream at night," a roommate says, "we'd all pile in Farrah's car and head for Baskin-Robbins. She was very generous with lifts."

In addition to ice cream sprees, Farrah liked to drive to Mexican restaurants. Her favorite place was Ernie's Chicken Shack, which looked exactly like its name suggests and was open, according to friends, "when the owner felt like it." There Farrah would feast on jalapeños, Mexican peppers fried like chicken and filled with cheese. More Burger, a hamburger joint, and various pizza parlors were other eating haunts.

Farrah was said by friends to have a cast-iron stomach—what there was of it. On one spring break a group of friends went to Acapulco where Farrah was promised the world—and definitely Mexico—by some wealthy admirer. She ignored his advances. Everybody returned from the trip with acute cases of Montezuma's Revenge. That is, everybody but Farrah who had been the bravest of the bunch by eating raw fish during the entire stay there. That same year at a post-victory steak dinner attended by football players and their girlfriends everybody got ptomaine poisoning. Again. Farrah survived the ordeal. "Greg called the next day," his sister Shanny recollects, "to say that the entire football team was on line all day outside the commode. I told him that we were in the same condition except for Farrah. We were crying from being so sick. Imagine, these big sturdy football players being felled by the meal, and Farrah is the only one in perfect condition afterwards." About the only time Farrah took ill was after her mother sent a shoebox filled with two dozen brownies with marshmallow icing. Friends say this had more to do with Farrah's head than her stomach. "She confessed the next day," Susan Parker remembers. "Farrah felt so guilty about not sharing the brownies. She always gave us some."

To everyone's amazement Farrah had a perfect figure. "Her legs didn't even have a dimple," one friend says. "They were as firm as a boys." For one week Farrah and her friends went on an exercise binge by thumping their thighs against the floor, but surrendered to complaints from neighbors below them. Farrah's famous hair also fascinated her friends. "Everyone else needed two hours just to roll their hair," Shanny Lott says, "but Farrah could shower, wash and roll her hair, and look gorgeous in less than an hour." She was equally quick about passing over compliments she received daily. "If Farrah would relate something nice a person said about her," Arden Westbook says, "she would do it in such a way that it would not come off as conceited and nobody was jealous."

Farrah's fitness was due in part to her being a gifted natural athlete. "She liked to do a lot of things other girls did not do," a classmate says. "Like hunting deer and duck. She kept up with the guys even on the tennis court." Shanny Lott remembers the time Farrah spent a skiing weekend at her family's cabin: "Dad took everybody on top of the mountain and told us to ski down it. Farrah was on my mother's unwaxed skis. She was the only one who did not fall down once. My hair was all messed up. Farrah looked like she had been combing her hair the whole time. Her hair just did what it wanted—and looked beautiful."

Farrah was also an enthusiastic dancer. She often attended fraternity parties with Greg, usually after a victorious football game. But they preferred to go with friends to beer joints like the End Zone which was equipped with bowling and pinball machines. Often a group of them would spend a Saturday night at Charlie's Playhouse and dance until nearly dawn to music provided by a local band known as the Mustangs. Mondays were amateur nights, and Farrah enjoyed listening to singers and musicians audition there.

Another favorite pastime was shopping. At least once a week Farrah browsed through Paraphernalia, a boutique that carried such mod fashions as Michael Mott and Betsey Johnson designs. "We shopped all the time," Shanny Lott confesses. "If it rained during the weekdays, we would forget about school. But a blizzard couldn't stop us from shopping on a Saturday. Though Farrah was much better than the rest of us about going to classes." Farrah bought Michael Mott satin-back crepe pants and tops in every color. Her closet was overflowing with clothes. Some of the mini-skirts and evening dresses Mrs. Fawcett generously and regularly sent Farrah remained, with price tags still on them, in the closet for months at a time. "We wore mini-skirts like bikini bottoms," friends admit. "And Farrah looked spectacular in them. Her legs were perfect."

Farrah and her friends decided that they would like to live in an apartment their junior year. Farrah, with her sweeping glance that can sum up a person or situation in seconds, scouted for it. Some people attribute her powers of observation to an artist's eye for detail. Driving about the perimeter of the campus, Farrah found an apartment complex shaped like a horseshoe—much like the Bay of Corpus Christi—built around a swimming pool. The building was still in the construction stage, and Farrah counted on her luck that it would be ready the following fall. She immediately signed up for a five-bedroom unit. As always, things worked out for Farrah. Further, with her friends from Mayfair House sharing the five-bedroom duplex, they could split the rent, which came to about $25 a person. "Leave it to Farrah to find the place," fondly recalls a roommate who today divides her time between selling real estate, teaching pre-schoolers, showing her art work, and maintaining a family. "We couldn't believe our good fortune at first. But then again, with Farrah everything always turns out the right way."

The apartment was instantly transformed into a social center. "There were the most terrific parties that the Univerity of Texas had ever seen," Shanny Lott exults. "Everybody who was anybody showed up." Kegs of beer were stacked up on the sidewalk out front and on the porch as an extra enticement. The parties, which became a weekend ritual, attracted a wall-to-wall crowd. Sometimes the apartment resembled a locker room because most of the women dated football players.

Friends remember that period as the most fun-filled time of their college years. Weekdays boyfriends and other classmates would sit around the living room and watch television together. The girls had rented a TV set for the apartment and considered it a treasure. Sometimes Farrah would sit atop it and perform for an admiring audience. In addition to her title as one of the Ten Most Beautiful Women at Texas, she was Navy ROTC sweetheart. But in the apartment it was her rollicking sense of humor that attracted rave notices. "Farrah could describe somebody hysterically," a roommate says. "She would tell a story that would have everybody in stitches, including herself. Farrah would slap her knees and just roar over something funny."

Comedy skits were their specialty. One memorable routine was the night Philadelphia Eagles football star Bill Bradley, then a student, and Texas quarterback James Street put on an impromptu skit. While Street posted himself in the bathroom, Bradley embarked on an elaborate introduction of this famous person who would magically appear on the spot. Street was to come on and do his Elvis Presley impersonation. But as Bradley talked on through the night, Street failed to appear. His prolonged absence evoked laughter of the kind that almost knocks people to the ground. "Farrah loved it," Shanny Lott recalls. "She laughed and laughed to the point where she was almost out of laughs. Then Bradley would begin again, with another glowing speech, and still no James. That would start Farrah laughing again." The girls got to sleep at close to dawn, and Street emerged from the bathroom to go home.

Sometimes Farrah, with an artistic temperament that usually served her well, was in no laughing mood. "The sweet darling," Shanny Lott says, "could go into a rage." One time when Farrah was furious with Greg, his sister says, the Angel jumped on top of him and started screaming and furiously pounding his chest. Another time at the Cotton Bowl in Dallas, after the University of Texas had a triumphant season, Farrah went into a temper tantrum after another girl said that she was after her boyfriend. Greg, amused by the accusation, unfortunately repeated the remark to Farrah. "She started screaming and hitting Greg in the parking lot," Shanny recollects. "Someone called the police to pull them apart. Greg, always delighted by Farrah in all her moods, held her close to him and tried to calm her down."

Farrah, with her fighting spirit, once turned her fury on an unwanted visitor to the apartment. Apparently a strange man was prowling the swimming pool at the apartment complex. Like a bloodhound he staked out his prey, namely Farrah and her friends. His first move was to make a scratching sound on the side of the building. Soon he graduated to the front door, an act that terrified the girls. Farrah, however, threw open the door and got rid of the intruder.

Farrah, who as Charlie's Angel regularly performs daring feats, could carry out most any detail during those years. Despite the fact that football players, with their characteristic lack of aesthetic appreciation, hung around the apartment constantly. Farrah managed to set aside time for her sculpting and painting. A major project was a sculpture of her boyfriend Greg Lott. His friends regularly checked up on the progress of the work, but such disruptions did not stop Farrah from completing it. In the end, the players put their jockery to good use. "The sculpture was so heavy," recalls Susan Parker, "that three of them had to carry it out of the apartment and lift it into a car."

Other pursuits proved less difficult. Somehow when the group planned parties, Farrah always wound up with the least arduous assignment. It was not by design, but just seemed to work out in her favor. While other girls scrubbed the floors and broke their fingernails washing dishes, Farrah was given the chore of buying dips and crackers at the grocery. "I can sometimes understand how the two other girls on 'Charlie's Angels' must feel," says Shanny Lott. "I saw a show with one of the women arranging file cabinets. Meanwhile Farrah was dancing and having fun on the job. This is exactly the way it has always been with Farrah. She must have a lucky star. Nothing bad ever happens to her."

Her life was, it seemed, made to order. But throughout her college years an offer that would one day alter the firm fabric of her existence loomed large. After she won the "Ten Most Beautiful" contest her freshman year, photos of Farrah and the other winners were sent to Hollywood. David Mirisch, a Hollywood publicist from the celebrated film family, gave Farrah his vote. He wrote and urged her to give up school and come to Hollywood. The letter was followed up by persistent telephone calls over the next year. "Farrah would say she was not interested," Susan Parker remembers. "Sometimes she wouldn't even mention that Mirisch had called until a few days later. Then she would say, 'Oh, that man called again.' "

Happy with her art work and devoted to Greg Lott, Farrah did not fantasize about Hollywood bringing instant happiness on the All-American plan. Others girls would have jumped at the chance to become a star, but Farrah had her life firmly planted in Texas. Not even the encouragement of friends could fill her with excitement about such a move. Susan Parker says that she told Farrah going to Hollywood would be great fun, a wonderful challenge. That pitch did not work either. Ironically, the man whom Farrah planned to marry played a key role in convincing her to snatch the Hollywood offer. "I will always respect Greg Lott for what he told Farrah," says Arden Westbrook. "He told Farrah that he wanted her to go to Hollywood. He said, 'Farrah, we can never get married if you don't know.'"

Always Farrah seemed to bring out the best instincts in people, including a boyfriend who risked the chance of losing her. "Her essence is that she inspires protectiveness in people," Arden Westbrook says emphatically. "This is not to be confused with helplessness." When Farrah eventually made a decision to go to Hollywood, friends, without any ulterior motives, went along with her. When one friend would leave, another would take her place. In short, they were devoted to her safety and well-being there.

Farrah, a girl who always had a sense of direction and purpose in her life, never imposed her own pressures on others. In the end it would be her own decision. "Farrah was a private person," Arden Westbrook points out. "She is really quite complex and introspective. She does not burden anybody else." Although Farrah lightly dismissed the calls from Mirisch, secretly she gave a good deal of thought to the offer. Yet the decision appeared almost effortless, as spontaneous as her fresh beauty. "We were sitting on her bed and watching the Academy Awards in the spring of our junior year," Susan Parker says, "and all of a sudden Farrah announced, 'I've decided to go to California'."

With an efficiency that allows Farrah to be a

successful sleuth in the employ of "Charlie," she went to Paraphernalia a short time after. "I want to look smashing because I'm going to Hollywood," Farrah is said to have told the manager. It was a line that Farrah had repeated many times before, and her wish had always come true.

Chapter 3

Farrah Heads for Hollywood

"You wanna come to Hollywood?"

The pitch was standard, but nothing about Farrah's arrival in Hollywood was a cliché. Instead of a sixty-ish movie mogul flying Farrah into town, her mother provided the transportation. Mrs. Fawcett drove her daughter the long distance between Texas and Tinsel Town. Even before they embarked on the journey, she had been given assurances that her daughter would be in good hands. In fact, Farrah had told the man who discovered her that she would have to check first with her parents. The Fawcetts made the necessary inquiries, and they were apparently satisfied with the answers, enough to entrust their precious daughter's career to someone they did not know personally.

That someone was Hollywood publicist David Mirisch. His credentials were impeccable. He was the scion of the oldest of the four Mirisch brothers whose motion picture career was capped by twenty-five Academy Awards. He himself had handled some 250 celebrities, and his current client list includes Lindsay Wagner, the Bionic Woman, who plays opposite Farrah's husband. "Farrah was really a sweet and innocent girl putting herself in my hands," Mirisch recalls. "Occasionally we did things socially like going to lunch or dinner. But I do this with any client. Nobody could ever say I tried to take her to bed."

Mirisch immediately checked Farrah into the Hollywood Studio Club, a sedate residence for women interested in acting or other creative careers. Its roster of residents had included such legends as actress Marilyn Monroe and writer Ayn Rand. South of Sunset, east of Vine, the three-story Spanish tile-roofed building, stuccoed in a splotched and faded terra-cotta, was ideally situated. Designed by still another talent, architect-engineer Julia Morgan who built, among other monuments, the Hearst Castle, San Simeon, it was considered a showcase for potential stars. The studio room, filled with Mediterranean-style furniture from the Hearst Castle, had a ballet bar and stage for movie reviews and variety shows. Until it shut down as a residence a few years ago, some 10,000 would-be and actual stars had slept there at least one night. Its motto, written on thick paper with an illuminated scroll border, told the story: "Hollywood—a major name to the ambitious career-seeking girl. To meet her needs for a home, friends, counsel and understanding, the Hollywood Studio Club was established in 1916 by the National Board of the Young Women's Christian Association."

The individual bedrooms, however, did not look very promising. Each room had a small bed, a sink, a white wooden vanity and matching dresser, and a closet. Shower stalls and bathtubs were communal. Some of the rooms were balconied and overlooked a Spanish-style courtyard lush with palm and banana trees. The rest were dark and almost depressing. All of them were cell-sized. Some girls would sleep on the porch and use their rooms to dress and put on makeup. Farrah, accustomed to her own apartment shared with close friends, was a stranger to these surroundings. Receptionist Ethyle Loring remembers her as less than ebullient: "She always had such a serious face. She was a very offish girl. Most of the others would stop to chat. Farrah never had much to say except a polite 'Good morning.' Now I don't know whether she was just bashful or didn't want to carry on a conversation. From looking at her today you wouldn't know it was the same girl."

Her days were filled with appointments Mirisch made for her with various television and commercial people. She started out by posing for different events in the area. Her photographs graced the pages of the Los Angeles *Times* as Queen of the Los Angeles Professional Tennis Championships and Miss Boat Show. "Unless a girl has strong professional talent and training," Mirisch explains with regard to Farrah, "you just take the beauty and run with it. You get her picture into the papers as much as possible, and you figure someone will see it and come up with a movie or television offer."

Mirisch recalls thinking that Farrah was even more beautiful in person than in photographs. "I saw her natural beauty in the photographs." he says, "but at the time she had not learned how to be aware of all the subtleties of the camera." He adds: "She wasn't just beautiful. She was extremely photogenic."

At the time Mirisch did not know where Farrah's career would lead in the end. "I don't think any of us ever have an idea where a young girl like Farrah is going," Mirisch points out. "My feeling is that there are a thousand Farrah Fawcetts—whether stewardesses or secretaries—and that the beauty of our land is not only in Hollywood. Farrah Fawcett got a break. Her break was that I found her and then persuaded her to come to Hollywood."

Before long there was another break, and Farrah made it. Through her lawyer she canceled her agreement with Mirisch six months after its inception. Today Farrah does not like to talk about it, except to say that Mirisch wanted 25 percent of her profits. Says Mirisch: "I was figuring 10 percent as her press agent and 15 percent as her personal representative. Whether she got it in one package or in two people she would have been paying the same amount." Along with the letter severing their relationship there was a check for his services, based on percentages, amounting to $210.46. "I never made a dime off her," Mirisch comments. "She wasn't making enough money at the time."

Today their paths rarely cross. But when Mirisch and Farrah do run into each other, both are cordial. One such time was at an Hawaiian golf tournament where Farrah was sunbathing by the swimming pool. Mirisch stopped to chat with her briefly. They saw each other again during a television awards program and talked in the studio green room. Mirisch's client, Lindsay Wagner, won "TV Personality of the Year" and Farrah got an award for "Most Promising." Mirisch and his former client exchanged a few congratulatory words.

"I am disappointed," says Mirisch, "that someone was able to turn her ear and make her have a letter written to discontinue the relationship." The negotiations were never done face-to-face with Farrah, and thus Mirisch can only speculate about her decision. He also theorizes: "She's only happened in the last year-and-a-half. If she had stayed with me, she could have happened a long time ago."

Clearly Farrah has happened. *She* is a happening! But the happening was not always happy. Farrah, whose reputation is as unblemished as her pristine beauty, warded off advances on more than one occasion. Susan Parker, a college roommate who moved from Houston to Hollywood to keep Farrah company and also have some fun herself, remembers: "Farrah had this toothpaste commercial, and she arrived home rather upset. She told me, 'This crazy man asked me to stand on a chair and see if I would or would not take off my shoes.' She was used to the womb of Texas. None of us had even heard about foot fetishists."

Susan's arrival in Hollywood meant that Farrah could move from the Studio Club to an apartment, now that she had a roommate. "It took two days for Farrah to find an apartment," Susan, whose mother also loaded up the car and drove her to California, recalls, noting her admiration for Farrah's apartment-hunting ability. She was also floored by Farrah's gift of memory: "The day I arrived, Farrah said that she had to go to the grocery store. A little while later she showed up with a big box under her arm. It contained a birthday cake. In the middle of all that we had to do, Farrah remembered that it was my birthday."

The new apartment was in a New Orleans-style building with its characteristic charm. It had four rooms. Located on palm-lined Horn Avenue in West Hollywood, a street just off famed Sunset Boulevard, it rises sharply into the Hollywood Hills. Looking down to the right lies the Sunset Strip, which in the 1960s became the mecca for many teenagers. Stenciled against the skyline to the left is the Shoreham Towers apartments, from which another aspiring actress, Art Linkletter's daughter, would later jump to her death in a drug-induced leap.

At this time Pauline and James Fawcett continued to live in Houston and were regularly helping Farrah out with her living expenses. They also kept in close touch, talking by phone with their daughter at least a few times each month. Pauline Fawcett would come to California to spend time with her daughter, and when Farrah returned home to visit, her mother would sometimes take her to the Four Seasons, an exclusive boutique in Houston's Westbury Square, to replenish Farrah's wardrobe. Friends say, "Whatever the Fawcetts had—and it wasn't all that much—they gave plentifully to Farrah."

By then Farrah had already met Lee Majors and was seeing a great deal of him. He played a big part in protecting Farrah from the indignities visited upon other young girls who came to Hollywood to become stars. Lee's personal agent played the same role for Farrah. Ironically, David Mirisch, whose office was in the same building as the agent, had intended to introduce Farrah to him earlier. His name was Dick Clayton, an articulate and sensitive man who today co-owns a film production company, Clayton Enterprises, with actor Burt Reynolds. Clayton met Farrah when she was riding with Lee in a golf cart he used to get around the studio. "She was so gorgeous," he recalls. "Who wouldn't sign her up?"

Understanding Farrah's strength and limitations. Clayton focused on assignments that would capitalize on her beauty and allow her time to develop as an actress. "Farrah had a light voice with a southern accent," he explains. "She was quite reticent about acting." Among the roles he got her were "Apple's Way," an ABC-TV series in which Farrah played the girl next door interested in tennis. She also did a few "I Dream of Jeannie" shows. Again, she had a beautiful girl part with one memorable line that went, "I have to change." A male actor replied, "Don't change too much." Roommate Susan Parker remembers that Farrah was highly amused by those lines.

Her amusement bespoke an ambition to get better parts. "I didn't want to give her anything way above her head." Dick Clayton explains, "because then she might retire into a shell and not want to try again. I avoided parts that would push her too hard."

As recently as last year, Farrah offered this assessment of her ability to George Howe of *Circus* magazine: "I don't delude myself about my acting talent. I know I'm not great. I wasn't blessed with that kind of ability, but I think I'm getting better. I think there's hope for me as an actress. You see, I'm basically a shy person."

Before Farrah was apotheosized in "Charlie's Angels," she decorated such television series as "Harry O" and the movie *Logan's Run*. Her first major movie was hardly a creative challenge. It took an emotional toll on her, though, and she regrets that she ever accepted the part. "It was a terrible film, but it taught me a lot about king-size egos and star trips," Farrah recalls. "All the performers were hung up on that, and I was the scapegoat on the set."

The movie was *Myra Breckinridge*, based on Gore Vidal's sex-change novel. Farrah played the girlfriend of a Cro-Magnon man and had the dubious distinction of having Raquel Welch try to seduce her. Once Myron (Rex Reed) transformed himself into Myra, Raquel Welch took over as Myra. There were tensions both on and off the set. Today, Farrah has replaced Raquel as the poster girl. Farrah's posters have broken all sales records, and Raquel has been relegated to a backstage position.

Of the *Myra Breckinridge* ordeal, Clayton sighs and says, "In this business everybody makes mistakes. This was mine, in getting Farrah the part." Looking back over the last year or two, Clayton commends Farrah for the strides she has made as an actress. "I have seen real improvement," he says. "But I expected it. Once Farrah made up her mind about acting she was tenacious about it. She really worked hard and gave it her best." After ten years of representing Lee and five as Farrah's personal agent, Clayton decided to devote full time to his own film company. But he remains attentive to their careers, and is happy and proud of their successes.

During her first year with Clayton, Farrah signed with a top commercial agent, Marge Schicktanz, then on her own and now with the William Morris Agency. Farrah was content to do commercials then. They met in 1969, and Marge helped her to become one of the hottest commercial properties. Farrah started with toothpaste and eventually cornered the hair conditioner market. Later she would get into cars like the Mercury-Cougar. In a good week of commercial-making today, Farrah can make about $30,000. A driving woman, Schicktanz went into high gear on Farrah's behalf and today the two of them have a mutual admiration society. "Farrah won't make a move," says one observer, "without checking with Marge."

It was not easy in the beginning. Roommate Susan Parker remembers: "At the time honey-blondes were in demand. Farrah was almost a silver-blonde, which was not 'in' then." Susan, who had been working as a secretary in the commercial department of a celebrity service, also felt on the "outs" in Hollywood. Her passion was back in Texas, and she returned to Houston to marry her childhood sweetheart. The year had been fun, and Susan was glad about having the experience of living and working in Los Angeles. Also blonde and attractive, Susan flashes a dimpled smile and says, "If I had become a movie star, I wouldn't have minded too much."

In a major feature on Farrah in the Dallas *Times Herald*, commercial agent Marge Schicktanz explained the initial difficulties of getting her client work: "The main problem with Farrah in the beginning was that they weren't using beautiful people anymore. I remember one car rental commercial we tried to get her. They wouldn't take her. They said they couldn't believe anyone who looked like that would be behind a car rental counter."

Assessing for the *Times Herald* how Farrah stacks up next to Ali McGraw, Margaux Hemingway, and Cybill Shepherd, all dazzling beauties who left modeling for indifferent movie careers, agent Schicktanz says: "Well, you really can't compare Farrah to them because they were all print models. Farrah has never been known as a magazine model. She's made her way in TV commericals and that's a big difference."

Then, with unwavering loyalty and protectiveness, Schicktanz is quick to add, "Plus, Farrah has got a lot of personality, a lot of coordination, and a great sense of humor. She's no dumb blonde."

Still uncertain in the early days about an acting career, Farrah's main interest, by all accounts, was Lee Majors. She spent a lot of time with Lee at his secluded Malibu home on top of a mountain. There he lived like an Ozarks resident, riding his horse down the hill to collect his mail. His companion was a German shepherd dog. A shy and sensitive man, he recognized Farrah's intrinsic beauty and vulnerability at once. Friends say that he was always looking out for her best interests and protecting her from possible hurts. He even added a room to the Malibu retreat, one friend remembers, so Farrah could have a place to pursue her painting and sculpting. It was an ideal relationship, and the view from his Malibu eyrie was perfect for a painter.

Farrah kept her own place at the start. When Susan Parker left, another University of Texas roommate, Arden Westbrook, showed up to take her place. It was like musical chairs. Arden took a job selling clothes at Saks in Los Angeles and eventually got into the music business. "We had fun," she recalls. "We ate hot fudge sundaes and drove around Los Angeles and giggled a lot."

Arden's arrival spelled another move, this time to a Middle Eastern style building topped with a minaret. Located on Olympic Boulevard near Beverly Hills, the building was shaped like a horseshoe, reminiscent of the formation of Corpus Christi Bay. The apartment itself had stained hardwood floors and a spacious dining room. "The landlady was a little old lady," Arden Westbrook fondly recalls. "She would come over all the time and ask us to roll her hair and drive her to the beauty shop. She was so dear that we always did what we could for her." On occasion the landlady could also turn grumpy: "She thought we had too many dates coming around the apartment, and this would make her real mad. She could be mean then."

Though Farrah was devoted to Lee, she always had a wide range of admirers including a movie star, known to be the local lothario, and a paraplegic at a hospital where Farrah and a few other young actors and actresses entertained once. Her college sweetheart Greg Lott visited Farrah briefly. But by then Lee was definitely the man in her life. According to Arden, the other actor, famous as a womanizer, saw Farrah emerge from Saks, pulled his car up to the curb, and recited his all-time line, "You are the most beautiful woman I have ever seen." From then on, for a few months, he would call at all hours of the day and night and would become enraged if Farrah was out. A favorite scenario was to talk to Farrah while allegedly carrying on a conversation with a United States Senator. "He tried to have Farrah believe that he was making major policy decisions for the country," Arden snickers. "He'd turn the phone in such a way that Farrah could hear his other lines ringing." Farrah did not buy his act. She was attracted to Lee's honest and genuine personality. The paraplegic also called and pledged his love to Farrah. She politely and gently avoided him too. "He wouldn't give up either," Arden sighs. "It was like college all over again."

After a year, Arden and Farrah called it quits as roommates. They parted amicably. Arden found another apartment in Beverly Hills, and they saw one another from time to time. "I love Farrah," she says, "and she will always be my friend. But I needed to be involved in my own world." Phone calls from agents and directors had been a round-the-clock element in Farrah's life.

An attractive brunette, Arden had been a model in the advertising department of Saks in Dallas before moving out to Los Angeles. As it had been for Susan Parker, the time spent in California had been fruitful and fun. She had become immersed in the music business. "If ever I had a stab at a career," says the twenty-nine-year-old Arden Westbrook, who today manages a Houston real estate concern, "it was then."

Like many girls with dreams of making it big in Hollywood, Farrah had also taken a chance by coming out to California. In fact, she had originally moved out as a lark, intending to spend only a summer and then return to her native Texas. But in the end she would stick with her career, be it good times or bad. "She was really introspective," Arden recollects. "But Farrah kept her pressures to herself. Her moods were inflicted on Lee. The only time I saw her cry was when she got upset over him. But I knew that she would be tearing her hair out over some of the things that happened during a routine day."

Farrah had a contract with Screen Gems, which two years ago became Columbia Pictures Television. She was paid $350 a week, in effect, to be trained. "They offered me acting lessons, horseback-riding lessons, all kinds of lessons," she recalls jubilantly. "I said to myself, 'Gee, this is terrific! I'll go back home when I feel like it.'"

It was Farrah's good fortune to be signed by one of the most extraordinary women in the business, Renee Valente, in 1968 head of the studio's New Talent Program and executive director of talent in charge of all casting for Columbia Pictures Television. A raven-haired, petite woman, who exudes authority and a strong intelligence heightened by a profound sensitivity about people, Renee Valente recalls, "It was fascinating how I came to sign her. It was almost unbelievable, like a fairy tale. I left my office to go down to the casting directors' floor below and suddenly I saw Dick Clayton (Farrah's agent then) standing next to this girl who was leaning over a desk and talking on the phone. I said to Dick, 'I don't care who she is or what she can or can't do. I want to sign her.' I did not even have her audition. It was the first time I had seen THAT person who would be the next Marilyn Monroe. Everybody thought I had lost my marbles. Sometime a bulb just goes on in your head—you know that you should sign somebody."

In designing the New Talent Program, Renee Valente was as prescient as she had been about Farrah evolving into a phenomenon. Farrah, along with seven others in the group, including Susan Howard and Christopher Stone, was given instruction geared to what could best be described as the "new person." Instead of the usual lessons in, say, dance, Renee Valente thought karate was a better way to teach coordination. Witness Farrah's feats on "Charlie's Angels" today! The acting coach was James Best, an actor in the greatest Western tradition. Farrah also attended one of his evening courses at a local college, and roommate Arden Westbrook went along. There may have been a hint of homesickness for Texas cowboy country. However, Farrah did not feel that she needed horseback-riding lessons and thus did not appear for them at the studio.

But Farrah took full advantage of the rest of the New Talent program. "In class she worked very hard," Renee Valente recalls. "I knew that she was never going to be Ethel Barrymore, but I never wavered from my conviction that the business would be ready for her." She adds that in 1970 Farrah had a part in a pilot that never aired. "If a network had bought it," says Renee Valente, "Farrah would have been a star then."

In 1971 when the entire industry underwent economic belt-tightening, Renee Valente called Farrah into her office to say that she would be kept under contract but that the coaching lessons would be cut from the budget. "You must promise me," Renee Valente told Farrah, "that you will take lessons on your own."

"In the most wonderful naïve way Farrah said, 'I

don't like lessons,'" Valente continues. "And she did not take lessons." Ironically, the studio head at the time was Leonard Goldberg, today at the top of the television production industry. In fact, with his partner Aaron Spelling, the two produce, among other hits, "Charlie's Angels."

"What few people realize," says Renee Valente, "is that with success comes security and with security comes a form of ability. There are some people who have the patience to learn theory and others, like Farrah, who don't. I believe, though, that Farrah will be a major star."

In addition to Farrah, another New Talent Program graduate, Kate Jackson, also stars in "Charlie's Angels." Kate Jackson periodically sends Renee Valente a bouquet of flowers with a note, "Just because I love you. Thank you." Actor Burt Reynolds also sent her a lighter with the inscription, "You make me believe in me," and the following year a plaque inscribed, "You still make me believe in me."

That someone like Renee Valente believed in Farrah from the start was in itself a tremendous boost to Farrah's career. Much like Farrah's mother, who displayed a great selflessness with regard to her daughter, Renee Valente has a reputation for nurturing stars she has signed—instead of milking them. She is a woman who is devoid of petty or jealous feelings. Though she herself climbed the traditional ladder to success, she does not begrudge anyone who in today's world does not have to struggle as long and as hard. She has been a pioneer for women in the industry.

The energy she expended in helping stars like Farrah has characterized her entire career. "If the kids had to learn karate," she recalls, "I would do the same. Anything I asked them to do, I would also do." Renee Valente started in show business by winning a dance contest at the Harvest Moon Ball in New York City. She danced in New York at the Chateau Madrid, the Latin Quarter, and the Tavern on the Green, and in Chicago at the Orchid Room. Then, tired of traveling, she decided to dance as an exercise rather than a career. She took typing courses and was instantly hired as a secretary for the Talent Associates firm of David Susskind. In no time, her skills—other than secretarial—became obvious, and she became a full-fledged television producer. Among the shows she produced were: "The Moon and Sixpence" and "The Power and the Glory." In 1960 she won an Emmy Award for the Art Carney Special, "VIP."

In 1964 Columbia Pictures Television (then Screen Gems) raided her away from Talent Associates as a producer for the company's international division. A year later she became director of East Coast programming, and in 1966 was assigned to produce the television series "Hawk."

The same year she moved to the West Coast to head the studio's New Talent Program, Farrah also arrived in Hollywood. And like superstar Farrah's meteoric rise to fame, Valente became vice-president of talent for Columbia Pictures Television in 1973. A well-integrated woman, with a husband, writer-producer Burr Smidt, and a fifteen-year-old son, Michael, who is interested in becoming a producer, Renee Valente continues to watch the careers of former New Talents. Of Farrah Fawcett, she says: "What I'm concerned about is that 'Charlie's Angels' is a wonderful training ground for

Farrah and it may be a little early for her to go out—unless the choice of material would be such that it would not make a giant stretch for her. We all know what timing means in the business. The difference is that Farrah is not just a flash-in-the-pan. Her look is 'in' and will be for some time to come, so Farrah could afford to wait a bit."

Buoyed by Lee's love and the professional support of agents like Dick Clayton and Marge Schicktanz, Farrah survived the initiation rites of the jaded industry without ever compromising herself. But above all, ambition and the willingness to work hard proved to be her anchor in this transient town.

For many young girls who fluttered around the fringes of the film world, Hollywood could be heaven or hell. Farrah was more than a survivor. She would become a superstar.

Ironically, Farrah reached the heights of stardom as an Angel and therefore for her Hollywood turned out to be heaven.

Chapter 4

Marriage for a One-Man Woman

On a bright weekend afternoon two women were shopping in a posh boutique in Houston's trendy Westbury Square. One of them was a handsome, well-dressed older woman; the other, in her twenties, was golden-haired. They got on so well, chatting and laughing as they went through the racks of clothing, that one would have figured them for friends instead of mother and daughter. As they stood around the counter while their purchases were being wrapped, the young woman remarked that she was returning to Hollywood to marry a big star. "I didn't think too much about it at the time," a clerk recalls. "A lot of girls came in and said things like that."

But Farrah Fawcett was not just any girl, and her husband-to-be, actor Lee Majors, was not the run-of-the-mill male in Hollywood promising to make every passing beauty a movie star. On July 28, 1973, they were married. The ceremony took place on the Swan Lake Terrace of the Bel Air Hotel in West Los Angeles. The palatial pink Mediterranean-style building, flanked by ferns and bougainvillea, overlooked a small lake graced by swans and assorted visiting waterfowl. It was a perfect setting for a couple attracted to the wholesome outdoor life.

The wedding invitation reflected their solid, almost old-fashioned values. Under a sepia-toned picture of Farrah and Lee was printed a quotation from the poet-philosopher Kahlil Gibran: "It is when you give of yourself that you truly give." The guest list included people from Farrah's childhood. She had remembered their decency and kindnesses. One of them was her dressmaker, and another was a woman who took Farrah to church when she was a small child. Neither of them was able to make the trip from Corpus Christi to Los Angeles, but they treasured the invitation and kept it as a souvenir. Farrah also had the good taste to leave her close friend Shanny Lott off the guest list. Shanny's brother, having once been pinned to Farrah, apparently had a substantial residue of feeling left for his college sweetheart.

It was a union as blissful as the warm July day. In Lee, this Catholic-bred Texan woman had met her ideal match. "Lee is close as you can get to Texas macho in Hollywood," friends say, not unflatteringly. "Huntin' and fishin' and playin' golf" was his idea of a good time. And the same could be said for Farrah, a vigorous and gifted sportswoman. At heart he was a country boy, and this appealed to Farrah, who always shied away from pretense. Neither of them had been through the Hollywood marriage assembly line. At seventeen Lee had married a woman who now lives in the south, and had a son, Lee, Jr., who visits each summer. It was Farrah's first marriage—but certainly not her first offer.

The couple had met the second week Farrah was in Hollywood. The same day his agent spied a Farrah Fawcett photograph, Lee left a terse message at the Studio Club, the all-girl residence where she lived during her first summer in Hollywood. The message: "Tell Farrah Fawcett that Lee Majors called and will pick her up at 7:30 for dinner." Besieged by men, like an invading troop, all her life, Farrah recalls reacting, "How dare he? Who does he think he is?"

Though Lee eschewed the flamboyant side of stardom, going so far, according to his press agent, as to pay to keep his name *out* of the paper, everybody knew who he was by then. A Kentucky boy, orphaned before he was two years old, Lee had gotten through Eastern State College on a football scholarship. But injuries (knee, shoulder, and a nose broken five times) precluded a pro career. He went west, hoping to become a high school football coach. But his first job was a recreation director at North Hollywood Park, an apparent spawning ground of stars. Alan Ladd was once a lifeguard there, and other athletically inclined actors would show up there to play football. After talking with them, Lee decided to try acting. So, after two years of studying and scrambling, by the time Lee courted Farrah he was already a star—Barbara Stanwyck's illegitimate son Heath on the hit ABC series "The Big Valley."

Before Lee came to pick Farrah up, he phoned her to apologize for his brashness. In an interview with Lois Armstrong, chief of *People's* Los Angeles bureau, Farrah remembers "melting into a thousand pieces" when Lee arrived and crooked his finger at her like a gun. "It was love at first sight, I guess," Farrah continued. "We got in the car and there was complete silence for about ten minutes. He didn't even ask me any stupid questions—like where did I come from. He said something once, but I couldn't hear it, so I just smiled."

Then harmoniously chiming in, Lee offered, "What I'd said was 'You're really beautiful'—and she missed it." They went to a discotheque where Farrah ordered Scotch and Coca-Cola, but didn't drink it. Instead she disappeared, under the weather, for thirty minutes. "I didn't know if she was really sick or if she just didn't like me," Lee added. The next day Lee sent her thirteen yellow roses. Their feelings did not wilt—they have been together for eight years since that day, the last four as husband and wife.

Farrah added the hyphenated Majors to her name. Other stars, like Patty Duke Astin and Lynda Day George, had added their husband's name rather than hyphenating it. "I took my husband's last name as part of my professional name because I'm so in love with him and also because I'm proud to be associated with him," Farrah told *Talk* magazine in November, 1976. "If I didn't think our relationship would last and be a lifelong, totally satisfying experience, I wouldn't have associated my personal name with my professional name."

In 1973, the year of their marriage, Lee was rewarded with his present series, "The Six-Million-Dollar Man," which has consistently been among the top twenty programs on A.C. Nielsen's popularity chart. This role was his final break—after playing the lawyer in "Owen Marshall"—from his Western-style image in "The Men from Shiloh" and "The Big Valley." It suited Lee. "It is probably the best thing that ever happened to TV," he says. "Kids haven't had a clean-cut all-American hero, and the Six-Million-Dollar Man is that kind of guy. I'm really humbled by that. This can lead them into good, basic all-American things like football. I think my image is good enough to uphold it."

It was that image, in real life, that attracted Farrah to Lee. Coming from the protected world of Texas and her parents, she suffered a bad case of culture shock in the brash, tough world of Hollywood. Her naïveté was apparent when right after shooting her first commercial a man involved in its production asked her out. When she turned him down, he warned her that he could keep if off the air if he so desired. "I told him he was a jerk," Farrah recalls. The commerical was never to be seen. Lee proved a buffer against such manipulations.

Though Lee, as the Six-Million-Dollar Man, has one telescopic eye and three nuclear-powered prosthetic limbs, he marvels at the creation that is Farrah Fawcett-Majors. "She's so gorgeous," he glows. "She's like a little girl. So cute, so beautiful inside ... you wanna ..." His natural reticence halts further elaboration.

His love for Farrah is so encompassing that anyone who touched her life in a small way, friends say, becomes important to Lee. On roommate Susan Parker's birthday, Lee took her and Farrah to a steak house on top of a mountain in Malibu, with a view of the star-studded sky and ocean, for a celebration. He gave another roommate a German shepherd puppy after his dog gave birth. And it is not unusual for Corpus Christi neighbors, who were good to Farrah as a child, to have autographed pictures of Lee. On a visit there to promote a bionic doll, Lee intended to visit with the woman who took Farrah to church as a child. His schedule was too tight that day, so he sent her a picture with a note thanking her for being so special to Farrah and promising to stop by the next time he was in town.

Roommate Arden Westbrook remembers the time, early in the Fawcett–Majors romance, that she called out to Lee's house on a weekend to tell Farrah that someone had called her about doing a commercial. Lee insisted, "Farrah is out here to rest!" Then he angrily hung up the phone on Arden. The following Monday afternoon, when Arden was alone in her office, she suddenly turned around and spotted a rose in a vase on her desk. "To this day I do not know how it got there," she says. "There was nobody around, and the place was completely still. And *there* was this beautiful rose." A note attached to it was her only clue. She opened it and read: "All we have in life are friends and family. Sorry about yesterday. Love, Lee." Sighing, Arden says, "Lee can be the dearest man. When he gets mad, he is an *enfant terrible* but he is really very sweet and shy."

Like most creative people, both Lee and Farrah sometimes have volatile tempers. Friends say that when either of them is angry, it is a wise idea to stay as far away as possible. Usually their fights would last a short time, and often Farrah would cry over Lee. "They are so in love with each other," friends say, "that it is only natural that they could be hurt by each other from time to time."

At the outset of their marriage, Farrah devoted most of her energies to Lee. Often during the day, when she was not filming a commercial, she would go over to his set and watch him work. Being together as much of the time as possible was a major goal of these two ambitious people. "Lee would come home exhausted," Farrah recalls, "and I would be full of energy, ready to go out. Now I know what it feels like to work that hard."

During those times, Farrah would take their meals into the bedroom because it was cozy with a fireplace there. "After we'd eaten," she told *Circus* magazine, "I would want to start doing the dishes, but Lee would say: 'Forget about them.' He'd want to kiss and hug and everything. When he finally got tired and wanted to go to sleep, I'd have to attack the dishes, which is the worst thing in the world for me. And that's how I talked Lee into hiring a housekeeper. I told him, 'If you want me in the bedroom, Lee, you'll have to get someone to do the dishes.' He hired a housekeeper the next day."

When Farrah signed on as one of "Charlie's Angels," in 1976, this cut into their time together. But from the start she vowed that Lee would always be her priority, and Farrah has not reneged on that promise. In fact, she had a 7 P.M. cut-off clause written into her contract so that she could arrive home in time to cook his supper. "That way," she told *People*, "he doesn't realize I haven't been home all day."

Initially Lee was not happy about Farrah taking

on such an arduous assignment as a television series. "He wasn't crazy about me getting into this business," Farrah admitted to *Circus* magazine. "He had these insecurities about 'Who is she working with?' But then, I had the same insecurities with him. So I figured if I had them, he should, too."

Husband Lee also had experience which proved to be invaluable to Farrah. Referring proudly to him as her "teacher," she says, "Lee is very happy and very proud of what is happening for me, just like I am for him. Besides, he has taught me a great deal—there's no competition because I consider myself on a different level of acting. I'm probably way beneath him in my mind ... and probably everybody else's mind."

Yet hard-working Farrah resents the suggestion that she coasted to fame on Lee's bionic trail. "I've been around for a long time," she says, with that Ultra-Brite smile that she flashes in the commercials. "Most people think I married Lee and then guested on his show a few times and that did it. But I've done quite a few things in my career."

Stardom has meant a big adjustment for Farrah, and Lee has been helpful in this area too. Once when Farrah went to the market with her natural hair puffed out and frizzed, a man came running up to her and said, "Oh, NO! What happened to your hair?" Upset by such a reaction, Farrah told Lee about it, and he explained everything. "Lee said that people expect to see me in a certain way, and I do understand this. Lee has been in the business eight years longer than I have. I'm still going through an adjustment period; it still comes as a surprise when strangers recognize me. But Lee is a big help."

Together the couple are a striking pair. Lee stands six feet one inch tall and has melancholy blue eyes. Farrah, with her sleek figure, flashes sparkling leaf-green eyes. At thirty-eight, Lee is eight years older than Farrah. Both of them are in the best bionic condition, and their bodies have resisted the extra layers other people gain every year after they cross the thirty-year-old mark. He is a Taurus which, Farrah jokes, sometimes make him a "grumphead." Her Aquarian nature is more upbeat and joyous. When queried about children, Lee quips, "We already have bids from people who would like pick of the litter."

Though Farrah would like to have some children around one day, both of them say they will wait a couple of years. "We were thinking of starting a family right away, and when we got notice that my series, 'Charlie's Angels,' was confirmed," Farrah told *In the Know*, "Lee said, 'Well, there goes another baby'." She told *Coronet*: "Stardom is probably like having a baby. No matter how much you prepare yourself for it, it's always a big surprise."

Farrah, whose own parents lavished affection on her, states emphatically, "I want to have time to spend with the child. I believe the first three years are the most important ones in a child's life." Her upbringing would surely prepare her for proper parenting. Lee, orphaned at a young age, has a special feeling about family and knows its value.

Farrah and Lee have reaped other rewards from their dual-career marriage. "When we come home, we have a lot to tell each other," she told *People*. "Mainly that we missed each other and that we're genuinely glad to see each other." Together they earn over a million dollars a year, and Farrah leaves the finances to Lee. His investments in "sure-thing" oil wells in Oklahoma and Kansas have been both wise and fruitful.

Many of her Tri-Delt sorority sisters married well-to-do physicians, and Farrah says, "If I were married to a doctor, I wouldn't see any more of him than I see Lee. And in my opinion being in the same profession has been good in our relationship. Whenever I come home with a problem, Lee's better equipped to understand it."

During the day they keep in touch by telephones installed in their his-and-hers Mercedes. "This is the only way we can talk when we're both working," says Lee. Each spends a minimum of fourteen grueling hours on their respective sets and arrive home in a state of near-collapse. The pressure was so great at one point that Farrah shed twelve pounds and more than a few tears. "By the time I get home, take the polish off my nails—they practically have to be done every day—I like to cook dinner for Lee if I'm not too tired," Farrah told *Coronet* magazine. "We usually take our meals into the bedroom and conk out early. That's why weekends and the times we're not working are so precious."

To illustrate how pressed their time is during filming segments of their series, Farrah recently cracked, "C'mon, Lee ... We have to take it when we can get it." Once inside the bedroom, of course, they tune in to each other's shows. "We watch his show more. He kind of falls asleep in mine. But I love his show. I never really think he's bad."

Home is a faultlessly decorated French Provincial eyrie overlooking a panoramic view of the San Fernando Valley. A sign at the bottom of the street, where about a half-dozen mansions are hidden behind hedges and iron gates, says PRIVATE PROPERTY. But fans have crossed out "private" and written "public" over it. While it can be approached by winding country roads, the house is only a few minutes from a freeway. And adoring admirers take the liberty of seeking out the house. But happily, the rustic byways are too narrow to accommodate the ubiquitous tour buses which both terrorize and haunt celebrities who choose to live on lower ground.

Fans of Farrah have emulated her talents as one of "Charlie's" sleuths and tracked down her parents' home twenty miles outside of Houston, in a country-club-like development built around a golf course. Frequently Farrah will call her parents and ask if it would be possible for her to rest there. Always eager to have their daughter home, they usually answer "Yes" and after a few minutes admit, "There are kids all over the place." The Fawcetts have an unlisted phone number, but people find their address and come by in person seeking autographed pictures of Farrah. Sometimes they just stuff their mailbox—which was stolen as a souvenir—with personal messages to their idol. While they are exceedingly proud of their daughter, Mrs. Fawcett says, "Since this show it has been terrible. It's about to drive me crazy."

As Hollywood's most famous lovebirds, Farrah and Lee have been unable to escape the gossip press. It bothers Farrah that her parents and friends have to read such sensational stuff about her. Routinely the gossip press terminates their marriage in banner headlines. The tabloid *Midnight* linked Farrah with eighteen-year-old Vincent Van Patten, whom they billed as a "bionic boy" because of his appearance on "Six-Million-Dollar Man" as a junior superman. As it turns out, Farrah and Vincent, son of comedian Dick Van Patten, are tennis buddies. Ironically, one of the pictures that accompanied the story was of Farrah with the whole Van Patten family, including Vincent's mother and father.

Farrah, once offered a Dear Abby-type piece of advice to young married couples on how to achieve a perfect marriage, says, "My life centers around Lee. I'm not ruthless or terribly ambitious, but I do want to get ahead with my career and do things that I consider worthwhile. In any case I don't place too much value on whether or not a film or television program flops. If it does, it's too bad, but my home life comes first."

Rumors of an impending breakup started after some paparazzi saw the two of them arguing in a Beverly Hills restaurant and snapped away. The argument instantly became a major national incident carried on the front pages of celebrity tabloids all over the world.

Lee, always protective of their privacy, tried to put a stop to the unfounded stories. He bought a full page advertisement in both the Hollywood trade dailies to tout an episode of his series that he had directed and then ended with a P.S., reading, "To quiet those rumormongers who are determined to dissolve our marriage in print, let it be known that Farrah Fawcett-Majors and I have never been HAPPIER in our seven years together."

Today they remain homebodies. They have a small group of friends, including Dinah Shore, who shares their interest in golfing, Rob Reiner, Penny

Marshall, and Johnny Carson. Both Farrah and Lee avoid talk shows because, he says, "Unless you're a singer or a comedian, you come off looking dumb." Friends say that Farrah's appearance on Johnny Carson several years back was occasioned by the fact that Wayne Newton, a friend, was guest-hosting the show. "Farrah probably did it for him," friends say. "Farrah was so shy that she didn't come across as herself at all. She must have been so nervous. She wasn't even funny."

A favorite retreat is in Arizona, on the shores of Lake Mead. The caretaker, Lee says, has probably never seen either of them on television. "It's in the middle of nowhere," he told *TV Guide*. "We sort of hide out there." Lee has a jeep and a boat for fishing trips. But, above all, they have privacy, which has become a cherished commodity in their lives.

Both Lee and Farrah are super-competitive jocks. Unhappily his image as the Six-Million-Dollar Man has restricted their activities in this field. Lee has taken himself off the celebrity tennis and golf circuit because, he told *People*, "I feel I'm a terrible disappointment if I miss a shot. Arnold Palmer does it, but the Six-Million-Dollar Man can't." Weekends Farrah runs two miles on the beach, and they enjoy fishing, hunting, and, on one occasion, skiing. "I'm up there on the top of the hill tryin' to stand up, doin' my bunny number, you know, the snow plow," he recalled in the *People* interview, "and here she comes, zip, zip. I haven't been back on skis since."

Farrah, who helped carry her team to victory in a bike relay during the ABC Battle of the Network

Stars a year ago, boasts mischievously, "On the tennis court we're very competitive. I KNOW I'm as good a tennis player as he." Then she coos, "Lee took me quail hunting. How many men could bring along their wives? I love to do the marketing," Farrah comments, "but I can't even go into the supermarket without forty people asking for autographs. We had to hire a houseboy to do the marketing."

Though Farrah has decided to stick with acting at last, reportedly a source of marital tension since Lee never wanted her to do this in the first place, she insists that he is and will always be her priority. A new commercial for President's First Lady Health Spas has just hit the tube, and Farrah has dropped the hyphenated Majors. But she explains, "Only when I have to say my name on camera will I do that. The whole thing is too hard to say."

Friends who read about rumblings of discontent in the Fawcett-Majors marriage say they do not believe a word of it. "People say Lee is lucky to be married to Farrah," Arden Westbrook comments. "But they forget to say how lucky Farrah is to have Lee, particularly in this period of cloudy sexuality. He is a real man!" Shanny Lott, whose brother lost Farrah to Lee and who would have loved to have her as a sister-in-law, frets over the gossip. "I don't know what Farrah would do without Lee out there in Hollywood," she says. "He is really important to her. He is strong and can protect her."

Farrah Fawcett-Majors, as she likes to be known, says, her eyes mellowing, "I like my marriage and Lee being the most important thing in my life. My

marriage is what sustains me, not just ratings figures or box-office receipts."

Clearly, Farrah does not need friends to remind
her—or rumormongers to tell her otherwise.

Chapter 5

Hair—
and Other Beauty Hints

The late afternoon sun shifted through the dining room of an apartment in one of West Hollywood's best-known older buildings. Totally Mexican in character and built around a courtyard, the stairs to each two upper apartments are tiled in a profusion of handmade plaques. Inside one of the upper apartments facing west with a view to the right of the hills, the mood is not of Spain, but pure Art Deco. A mirage of color, from the muted cocoa walls, the foil for priceless Imari plates, to the Chinese carpet in red make a daytime room as sophisticated as the pearl gray couch. In the twilight, as the room darkens and the lights are turned on, it becomes naturally mysterious with a myriad of lights reflected in the beveled edges of the mirrors. A warm, restful place, it is in total contrast to the ebullient temperament of its owner, hairstylist Hugh York.

"We go back seven years," Hugh says of Farrah. "Seven years ago, she said, 'I don't know what they want,' and I'd say, 'Farrah, they want you just to go out there.' "

If the Farrah look can be attributed to anyone, then it can be said that it was created by Hugh York, for he was the person who in 1970 first cut her hair, just the way he cuts it now. And it was he who changed her look from all one color to the streaked mane that is her mark.

At thirty-three, Hugh York is at the top of his profession. Well over six feet and also eminently photogenic, he emanates an earthy sophistication. Something very real.

"That's what I really love about Farrah—her honesty," he says. "She's truthful and doesn't play games. She realizes what business is about. She's 'in' and she knows it. A real pro. But don't get me wrong, *she* created her existence. If I hadn't cut her hair that way, she would have found what her look was all by herself. Farrah really knows who she is."

Hugh York can well be said to know who HE is. Born in Scottsdale, Arizona, in the 1940s, Hugh was the only child of a rancher who raised Black Angus cattle. He came from a background as unspoiled as Farrah's. "I didn't know my dad was rich," Hugh recalls, "until one day I went with him to buy a Caterpillar tractor for the ranch, and he paid for it by peeling off $30,000 in bills."

When Hugh was seven, his parents gave him his first taste of independence—in the days before jets his mother put him on a plane to meet his father in New York. He managed to get lost in Salt Lake

City while reading a comic book during a refueling stop, but it was seven-year-old Hugh who reassured the frantic airline officals using the words his mother said when she kissed him goodbye: "You'll be fine, Hugh. You're insured." The same strong sense of self that Farrah's close family background gave her, brought Hugh to Hollywood in 1969.

After Farrah's parents agreed that she should choose her own course and she left college to go to Hollywood, her father told her she would have to get a job, and took away her credit cards. That may have been one of the more traumatic moments of young Farrah's life. "It was," she told US magazine, "a rude awakening. I thought you bought everything with a credit card." Other financial matters like income taxes also left her confused. "I kept getting these W-2 forms from employers," she continued in the US interview. "I had never seen them before. One day my father said, 'You are getting someone to take care of your income tax, aren't you?' I told him I thought he was doing it. He got very upset with me."

When Farrah and Hugh met, she had just filmed *Myra Breckinridge*, an image she wanted to shed immediately. "She was in a transition period," Hugh recalls. "The filming had been a miserable experience. She was ready for something to happen."

At the time, her hair was one color and basically one length. "The look I gave her moved out of the bleached and toned hair to highlighted hair," says Hugh York. "It was totally new but at the same time it was very difficult because streaked hair showed badly on film. What I saw for Farrah was a streaked image that was softer, with that great face and studiously casual clothes. It's a charming, real look, and that charm comes through."

Hugh York also gave his client a new way to handle commercial filmmakers: "If they squeak about the streaking, just tell them, 'You bought it this way, just take it. You bought it, take it!' "

When THAT HAIR was created, it was in sharp contrast to the look of the day—the more geometric hair cut which was popular at the time, or the straight Alice-in-Wonderland look.

Hugh York says that Farrah was one of the first girls to have her hair highlighted because of the difficulty it creates with filming. But then Farrah was used to being first. She was a trend-setter in the way she dressed at college back in Texas, and she really saw her look and stayed with it.

After filming *Myra Breckinridge*, Farrah continued to do more and more commercials. Pretty girls were standard fixtures on the set, but a really beautiful woman with a look all her own was something new.

"Farrah's hair at this time was almost a pastel pink bordering on pink silver," Hugh York remembers. "It was a dumb blonde and cutsey-chick look, just like the lines they would give her to recite."

"I told Farrah," he continues, "that it's over—unless you want to be categorized as a dumb blonde. If you want to do comedy, fine. Keep that hair and you'll keep getting those lines. But who wants to look like that?"

Always an individualist, Farrah wanted to have her own style. "If she hadn't been ready for a change and if I hadn't done it," Hugh York emphatically states, "it would have happened anyhow. Farrah was ready and if she hadn't been then she would have done it on her own. She created her existence."

During this period Farrah worked on a few commercials in Mexico. To this day she was never paid, but still gave it her all. "She did some incredible work creating her own existence," Hugh York says. It was building her look and her career.

Always willing to work hard and knowing where she was and wanted to go, Farrah did not want to be forever at the mercy of directors who would give her the standard comeback: "You were fabulous. You just gave the best reading and we love you—but could you just bleach your hair." Once Farrah decided that she had had an earful of this kind of talk, Hugh York assured her, "Farrah, now that you have YOUR look, you'll never be dubbed a dumb blonde."

What happened was that Hugh York moved her over with THAT LOOK—out of "Let's get that cute blonde," to the Farrah Fawcett look. "I gave her the image but she created the look," Hugh York explains, "and it did take five years. Consider what she was doing at that time: loads of commercials, of course, but until 'Charlie's Angels,' not too much acting work. Take for instance when, after Lee soared as the Six-Million-Dollar Man, Farrah had a couple of guest spots. She wasn't that good. Maybe she was intimidated because it was Lee's show or maybe the director was intimidated. The line between selling a product, which is a walk-through for Farrah, and acting is very rigid."

Hugh York elaborates on this theme: "If you get Farrah within five feet of a camera she's incredible in the commercials—toothpaste, a car, hair conditioner—she just comes alive, and that's the toughest acting of all. But straight acting is different. For her it's contrived and because of her naturalness she had to work at it."

His apartment fills with tawny light as the sun goes down. The kitchen is crowded with personal treasures, a six-burner gas stove from the 30s bought at an auction—and it works, he says gleefully. His refrigerator is topped by a signed glass dome on an inlaid French base, probably designed to house a stuffed mechanical singing bird. But Hugh has it filled with corks from wine and champagne bottles he has shared with friends. "They are all signed, all real and all mine," he beams. "That's one of my favorite things in this apartment."

It is Hugh's childlike appreciation for freshness and beauty that must surely have drawn Farrah to him. They have remained friends as well as being professionally involved from the moment they met in 1970. Hugh York says that Farrah in person looks the same as on the screen. "Great hair, great skin, and these beautiful eyes."

Farrah's eyes are really played up on "Charlie's Angels," but off the set Farrah just wears a little beige overlay on her lids and a light mascara. Her eyes, depending on the light or her mood, are deep green or a lovely leaf-green. On the set different-colored eyeshadow really brings out her eyes. Grape shadow on her lids makes the green highlights more apparent. A dove gray makes them almost navy blue. Farrah has never worn false lashes. With her long, silky lashes she doesn't ever need or use heavy mascara. Farrah simply brushes the upper and lower lashes two or three times for emphasis.

Elisabeth, famed makeup artist and face treatment specialist of the Elizabeth Arden Salons in

Beverly Hills, California, and Milan, Italy, claims that anybody with eyes as sparkling as Farrah's needs only a hint of assistance. She should know. She works with Arden's Pablo when he is demonstrating and offering consultations at $35 for fifteen minutes. Cleansing old makeup off the eyes each night before bedtime is most important, according to Elisabeth, and using eye-makeup remover soaked into a cotton pad will nourish that delicate part of the face overnight.

For this summer, Elisabeth recommends, anyone wanting to get a look like Farrah—fresh, outdoorsy, and quietly sexy—should be mindful of the newest colors. After all, Farrah is the NEWEST look. Poppy tones for lip gloss and blusher can be complimented by eyeshadows in subtle and soft ash browns for a basic color, good for everyone. For green eyes use taupe-stone greens; for olive skin plum-wine shades because eyeshadow will pick up the poppy rage and give a soft look. And for big brown eyes, use cinnamon tones for shadow.

Remember on weekends and during the day, like Farrah, no mascara for the girl who runs two miles on the beach whether it be Malibu or Corpus Christi. "I tell all my clients to cleanse their face thoroughly morning and night," says Elisabeth, who takes care of the skins of many American and European beauties. "I even have teenagers as clients, and their mothers are European-born and insist on good skin care from the start." American women, she adds, do not take care of their skin, and this is why she believes Farrah has a tremendous influence on facial care. Clear, clean skin is the basis for Farrah's all-year-round summer golden-girl look.

For the evening the look in eyes for the summer

of '77 is more smoky. Still color, but color that is buffed down, says Elisabeth, more smoky. Big colors are Sherwood Forest green and slipper blue, and the crayon color pencils are great for getting that soft Farrah Fawcett look for the eyes.

But back to hair! Hugh York reflects that there has never been an actress remembered for her hair. "Farrah's hair is the Shocker, the Flasher!" Looking back star-wise, Hugh offers, "You may remember Joan Crawford's shoulder pads or Veronica Lake's peek-a-boo hair which covered half her face so that she only showed one eye. Abbe Lane had a mop of red hair pulled back. Tallulah Bankhead had a thick copper-colored mane—but that was offset by everything else she had going for her. Garbo had great hair, but it was overshadowed by her presence. Jill St. John had a hair image for a year or so and so did Twiggy. But no one has utilized her hair like Farrah. With other stars you might remember a lip line (Paul Newman), a mouth (Sophia Loren), breasts (Jane Russell), or a wiggle like Marilyn Monroe—but no star has been remembered just for her hair. And that's Farrah! Her hair!"

Hugh York is emphatic: "Length is what men love. Farrah has fantastic hair—just curly enough, just the right amount of wave. It falls about two inches below her shoulders. But let me tell you, she works on that look. You can't get a look like that unless you maintain it. Her hair is not too thick or too thin and has good body enhanced by the streaking."

Then flashing his huge, curious, blue-green eyes, Hugh exults, "Farrah's hair is magic. It makes her the fantastic person she is." And what is a fantastic person in 1977? Well, Hugh York says, "A fantastic person means you can be a major symbol in today's society. And Farrah certainly is THAT!"

Hugh York says that THAT HAIR is Farrah's identity. Even other celebrities could not wear the FF look. "Imagine Shirley MacLaine with a Farrah Fawcett hairstyle?" Already a major Los Angeles department store, the May Company, advertises "Angel" wigs—"to get the look you want." But a wig won't do it, because the whole story behind THAT LOOK is the movement of Farrah's hair. Free, unbound, windblown. And there's feeling behind it. The Farrah Fawcett look has flourished all over the country. Besides the hair, it's that fresh sporty feeling that really spells 1977.

Hugh York's career has been crowned by a collection of celebrities who are his clients. In New York, for example, his list includes such names as Candice Bergen, Cheryl Tiegs, and Margaux Hemingway, and in California he tends the tresses of such stars and models as Pam Grier, Suzanne Pleshette, Elizabeth Ashley, Mrs. Sammy Davis, Jr., Ursula Andress, and singer Esther Phillips. Hugh also does the hair of studio executives, their husbands and wives. He has cut Lee Majors's hair and the hair of super-singer Neil Diamond.

Before moving to California in 1969, where, like Farrah, he seemed to happen at the right moment, Hugh York freelanced for *Vogue, Harper's Bazaar* and *Glamour*, and worked with such famed photographers as Irving Penn and Richard Avedon. He also had a direct line to the Eileen Ford Model Agency. A lover of beautiful women, Hugh calls Farrah "not just a fantastic beauty but a sensational one." Married three times, Hugh York says that he is most successful in a relationship with a woman when they just live together.

Ironically, it was Hugh York's free-form training that has characterized his career. When he was fifteen he went to San Francisco to stay with some aunts; he cut and set their hair, and that of some of their friends. Recognizing that he had a natural feel for hair, they quickly set him up in a salon. Like Farrah, Hugh eschewed an assembly line approach to beauty. "Hairdressers tyrannize women," Hugh York says, and then adds as a question, "How many times have you been messed over by a hairdresser trying to impose his or her own will on to yours? 'Oh, but you'll look simply terrific' and you wind up looking like the 'before' picture on a make-over story."

Hugh York who arrived in Hollywood via New York when he was hired as Candice Bergen's hairstylist for the film *The Sand Pebbles*, says of Farrah: "All I wanted to do was utilize her hair so that it would work like her personality—it moves and it has feeling. It surpasses Farrah—the feeling."

Unlike many superstars, known to throw temper tantrums both in and out of the hairstylist's chair, Farrah behaves in an unspoiled, considerate way when Hugh York is doing her hair. "She's really wonderful and bright," he says. "The only time she gets upset is when the phone is ringing and it's her attorneys or agents. But she never takes it out on me. She just politely says, 'Excuse me, I just have to take care of this.' She is very smart about business—even with people pulling at her from all sides."

Such a beehive of activity would be enough to make lesser stars fall apart. But not Farrah, who is unflappable even in the most frantic of times. Like her lustrous hair, everything seems to fall into place in her life.

Hugh York, whose hair is silken brown with a matching beard, says the bottom line is that Farrah knows herself and her hair. "Farrah knows she has a manufactured look," he says. "She knows she is packaged like other stars. But the incredible thing is that she is so natural about it, with it. The clincher was when she became Farrah Fawcett-Majors. She really likes to have her hair wet and pulled back or blowing in the wind. That's Farrah!"

It is also like Farrah to come to Hugh York instead of having him go to her. "If Farrah wanted me to come up to her house," he says, "I would do it for her. But she has always come by my shop." This fall York intends to open his spiffy salon, Hugh York, at another jazzy address, Sunset Boulevard and Sunset Plaza, just off the Sunset Strip. Though Farrah finds it hard to go anywhere without becoming surrounded by fans, she would not have that problem at Hugh York's salon. Like Farrah, he is enormously private, and he extends this courtesy to his clients. "Nobody," Hugh York declares with firmness, "would bother anyone who came to my salon." And he means it.

Farrah's hair is a treat to work on, Hugh York says, because she knows what she wants and doesn't change her mind every five minutes—or five years. "If she is working on a set and does not have her hair absolutely the way she likes it—if she doesn't feel the energy," Hugh York explains, "she'll say, 'Excuse me, I need twenty minutes,' and then she returns with her hair looking exactly like she wants it to."

Keeping her hair the way she wants it to look can be as exacting as the motions she goes through on the set. "If Farrah is working, hairstylists on the set may comb her out every twenty minutes. Sometimes she'll sleep in rollers. Farrah has fabulous hair. But it doesn't just happen. She works, like she does with everything, to maintain it."

Hugh York's bathroom, with its Spanish arched doorway, is papered in an apricot-taupe Moroccan geometric design. With a tortoise split bamboo shade like the window coverings in the kitchen, the rest of the bathroom picks up the apricot of the walls. There is a monogramed HY bathmat and bathsheet hanging over the walk-in shower. To the right of the shower and next to the sink is an African basket full of beige towels rolled tight like logs and stacked on end in the basket. The mood is at once luxurious and fun. The rest of the bathroom is sparsely done with only a few other accents, echoing the famous "more is less" style of decorating: a porcelain dish for soap and a small bamboo table. The effect is immaculate.

"Hair must be kept clean," says Hugh York, whose well-cut fingernails are spotless. "Farrah washes hers as much as it needs to be washed to look her best." Often after a day on the beach, Farrah's hair will glow like strands of sunlight. But the sun can also do damage, and the all-knowing Farrah knows how to repair it. It is the fabulous Farrah, in fact, who does commercials for her hair conditioner, Wella Balsam. She uses that product along with others.

To maintain hair, Hugh York says, you have to use different kinds of conditioners, whether cream or protein. After a while, the same conditioner

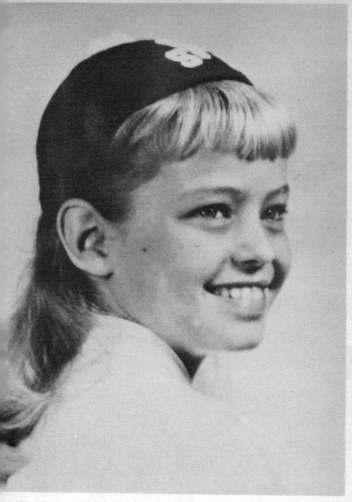

Farrah, a third-grader at St. Patrick's in Corpus Christi, Texas, wears a beanie as part of the school uniform.

Farrah's photo as the Most Beautiful Girl at W. B. Ray High School appeared in the 1965 Silver Spur yearbook.

In her first modeling job for her high school art teacher's evening class Farrah refused to wear a bathing suit like other models.

The ever-popular Farrah cavorts with friends at a University of Texas gathering.

Farrah with University of Texas football player Greg Lott, who was her college sweetheart.

Upon arriving in Hollywood, Farrah's picture appeared in the local papers as Queen of the Los Angeles Boat Show.

Farrah also stayed afloat in the public eye in 1968, as Miss Pro Tennis.

Farrah and Lee's wedding invitation was done in sepia-like tones with a message from Kahlil Gibran.

Farrah Fawcett becomes Farrah Fawcett-Majors after her marriage to Lee Majors. PHOTO: BRUCE MCBROOM/GLOBE PHOTO

Farrah and her mother, with whom she remains close today, pose for a wedding party picture. PHOTO: BRUCE MCBROOM/GLOBE PHOTO

Hairstylist Hugh York and his client Farrah. Hugh gave Far-rah The Look. PHOTO: DOUGLAS KIRKLAND/COURTESY OF HUGH YORK

Farrah relaxes on the set in her trailer. PHOTO: TONY COSTA

Farrah, sporting her famous $9,000 fur coat—financed by her fee for doing a spot on "The Captain and Tennille," steps out with husband Lee Majors. PHOTO: KEN REGAN/CAMERA 5

Director Allen Baron shares the spotlight with Farrah and her co-Angels on the set of "Charlie's Angels." PHOTO: COURTESY OF ALLEN BARON

In Bosley's living room, where the Angels meet for strategy sessions, Farrah flashes a devilish smile.
PHOTO: JULIAN WASSER

On the set of "Charlie's Angels" Farrah takes a break from the camera. PHOTO: JULIAN WASSER

At the Battle of the Network Stars Farrah pauses reflectively between matches. PHOTO: KEN REGAN/CAMERA 5

Farrah, a top tennis playe

isplays a belligerent backhand and a ferocious forehand.

"This is the real Farrah," her friend Shanny Lott says. *Farrah sent her the picture.* PHOTO: COURTESY OF SHANNY LOTT

would be rejected by the system once it absorbs too much of one kind. So Farrah switches hair potions like everybody else. But everyone needs conditioner. Short hair, long hair, natural hair, streaked hair like Farrah's.

"Her hair is medium thick and the streaking gives it more body. Unless Farrah wants it to grow longer than her normal length," Hugh York advises, "she gets it cut every six weeks or so. Everybody should have their hair cut that often. It's healthy for the hair." On a day-to-day basis, when Farrah is working on segments of "Charlie's Angels," she will set her hair herself in hot rollers or have hairstylists on the set do it. "Hot rollers are not harmful to the hair if used once a day on healthy hair," Hugh York points out. "But more than once a day on hair requires paper on the ends of the hair before using rollers."

Any woman who thinks that a cut like Farrah Fawcett's will instantly give her THAT LOOK, cautions Hugh York, is just fooling herself. Hugh York, a workaholic who revives himself at night to go on the party circuit, says that if a woman gets a Farrah Fawcett cut at 2:00 P.M., she would need, if she is going out that night, to put hot rollers in around 8:00 P.M. and probably give the hair a comb-out by 10:00 P.M. But, he adds, "Overwork will ruin it. It's important not to try to set it too together. That's the magical part of Farrah's look—no matter how hard she works at it, the hair does not look like a major effort."

In trying to approximate that FF-M look, Hugh offers some pointers:

1. Bend the head over and brush out the hair.
2. Throw back the hair.

3. Pick the pieces out of the face.

4. Straighten out the length.

Everybody wants to look like Farrah Fawcett-Majors. That includes mothers, daughters and even long-lost aunts. "They want that movement, feeling," Hugh York says. "Farrah's image is that she moves from a male standpoint, and she moves from a female standpoint. It's identifiable to everybody."

If this be the case, then wipe off the fingernail polish. Farrah herself went through the whole patty-nail, porcelain period. Up until last year, Farrah's long nails were polished, but now she has switched to clear polish. Shorter, clean nails, which are her own, have that natural look. "Farrah has very slender, sensitive, sexy hands," Hugh York says, "and the clear polish enhances them."

Her toenails are untouched. Again, this is in keeping with her *au naturel* spirit. On weekend beach runs, Farrah goes barefoot or in sneakers for tennis. Hugh York says Farrah is competitive, athletic, on the go, on her feet a lot of the time. Friends say her feet are so square that Farrah could stand on her toes like a ballet dancer. In short, toenail polish does not match her image. "The majority of what is done to Farrah is by Farrah, for Farrah, and because of Farrah," Hugh York says.

Being outdoors whenever she can, Farrah loves the sun. She keeps a luscious golden-bronzed color. "She doesn't overdo it," Hugh York says. "She's cautious. She uses a sunscreen." Assuredly Farrah lubricates her skin so that it stays soft and silky instead of leathery.

The Farrah Fawcett look spells Total Care. The clean shiny hair tops a tailored look. And the 100 percent girl wears the 100 percent look. Whether it's 100 percent cotton shirts and denims, or 100 percent wool pants. Although Farrah is quite tiny, around 5 feet 6 inches with no more than 112 pounds on her gorgeous frame, she appears tall and leggy on the screen and in magazine pictures.

Her hair has such versatility that it looks good with both tailored and slinky, sexy outfits. She alternates easily between sundresses, Calvin Klein T-shirts, and man-tailored wool blazers. On one show Farrah wore the most popular Stanley Blacker blazer of the Spring 1977 collection. A tweed number with suede patches on the elbows and leather buttons, it was instantly a sell-out in every smart women's haberdashery on the West Coast.

Above all, the hair gives Farrah stature, a special identity as a star. "Farrah's hair is soft. It moves," Hugh York gushes. "It's touchable, believable."

"Farrah," chorus her fans, "don't change a hair for us."

Chapter 6

Charlie's Angels

"The worst job in the entertainment business is being a star of a television series," veteran producer Barney Rosenzweig says. "The only thing worse is being a female star. Starsky ['Starsky and Hutch'] can show up unshaven and with bloodshot eyes and his clothes rumpled. But the women have to look perfect, with their hair done and in beautiful clothes."

Happily, Rosenzweig was the producer of eleven segments of the hit series "Charlie's Angels" last season. "We were fortunate," he sighs, "because all the girls are beautiful, so we don't have to shoot through Coca-Cola bottles or gauze."

Like her two co-Angels, Farrah looks like she does not have a care in the world. Despite a schedule that would send most people to the recovery room of the local hospital, Farrah is always fit.

Perhaps being an Angel leaves little or no time for the kind of reckless living that causes creases under the eyes of other women.

As one of Charlie's three Angels, Farrah gets plenty of action on the set. The trio risk their gorgeous hides as sleuths for a private detective, Charlie, who has such a penchant for anonymity that he is never seen on the screen. Usually Charlie is too busy dallying—in double entendres—with other luscious women to do more than just state the case. His go-between is a bumbler named Bosley (David Doyle) who provides comic relief for the scrapes that threaten the lives of these gun-toting beauties.

Clearly the Angels are the apple of America's eye. Every Wednesday night at 10:00 P.M., EST, 50 percent of all TV sets in the United States are, according to *Time*, tuned into them. Translated, this means that in 23 million households people are gazing at these superstars. And what a sight they are to look at—sexy Farrah Fawcett, sweet Jaclyn Smith, and smart Kate Jackson. Though all three Angels have soared in popularity, it is Farrah who has emerged as the most popular. Apparently this has not damaged their relationship, which is one of mutual respect and liking. "I've been in this business a long time," says Rosenzweig, who in the past nine years has produced over eighty hours of prime-time television as well as independent theatrical feature films. "I've never seen a better rapport."

Says Farrah: "The only time we have an argument is when we're all racing for the doughnut tray." On Kate's birthday Jaclyn ordered a cake with three dolls in it—one blonde and two brunettes.

In the original guidelines for the show, then line-producer Rick Husky wrote at one point:

"What we have is Angie Dickinson ['Police Woman'] times three." The characters of the Angels were tailored to the exterior attributes of each woman. Though the Angels insist that their roles are pretty well defined, producer Rosenzweig says that lines written for one Angel may be assigned to another. Thus their versatility as actresses comes into play.

Herewith their roles as initially drawn up by Husky in what is referred to as the "bible" of the series:

Jill Munroe
(Farrah Fawcett-Majors)

A California girl with cover girl looks, Jill is gorgeous, open, warm, romantic, a bit kookie. She wears her heart on her sleeve, and since her heart beats within a lovely bosom, men all over the place are eager to be the recipients of those ready emotions.

The most naturally athletic of the trio (though they are all *athletic*), Jill is dynamite on a tennis court, in a bikini, or scaling the side of a six-story building. And that athletic ability she readily admits has been inherited from a sports-crazy family: a mother who was a tennis pro; a father who played minor league baseball. The odds on tomorrow's game, the Super Bowl, the World Series? Jill is Jimmy-the-Greek with curves, a veritable encyclopedia of sports knowledge and trivia, and has been known to pause in the midst of a hectic investigation to place a wager on a long shot at Santa Anita (with invariably good results).

Jill has a small house at the beach, leads an outdoor life off the job, is devoted to her family, and digs country-and-western music. Her relations with the opposite sex are active, California free, with her love of men equal to their love of her. Marriage? When the right man comes along, according to Jill. But not right now. She's having too much fun.

Obviously Farrah is sexy, athletic, and out-doorsy. But she's Texas-bred and wed to the Six-Million-Dollar Man. "It's a little hard to go home to the mamma," one stagehand admits and then adds, "I'll bet there's not a guy on the set who doesn't have a mad crush on her." And there is much more to this gorgeous gal.

But the show must go on ... so here's ...

Kelly Garrett (Jaclyn Smith)

Kelly is radiantly beautiful, silkily sophisti-cated on the outside but the most sensitive of the trio on the inside. Born and raised in Hous-ton, Texas, and a touch of that Texas drawl still peeks through now and then. While her past is not as shrouded in mystery as that of her boss, Charlie, there does seem to be more to Kelly than meets the eye; something deeper, hurt from the past, that makes her react more emotionally to situations than the other girls. A model for Kelly's character might be the Peggy Lipton characterization of "Julie" in "Mod Squad."

Of the three Angels, Kelly would be the more cynical. She's not hard, but she's streetwise. Orphaned early in life, she's been around, worked as a stewardess, a cocktail waitress in Las Vegas, etc. Kelly thinks twice about everything she does, and, since she's heard every "line" invented, she's not quick to accept anything on face value. Also, she's the most adept at self-defense and an expert on the police pistol range. Anyone who's tried to tangle with her has quickly discovered those curves are dangerous.

Kelly lives in a small canyon house with a large standard poodle named Albert, who thinks he's a German shepherd. She's crazy about animals, is a mother to every stray pet imaginable, and collects them like some women collect clothes.

The quietest of the Angels, Jaclyn is the daughter of a Houston dentist and his wife—"the sweetest people I know," she told *People*. She was even closer to her maternal grandfather, a minister, who died at the age of a hundred and one. A self-styled "old-fashioned" girl, Jaclyn lives alone in a Tara-style house in Beverly Hills which she has furnished with antiques. After studying drama at Trinity University in San Antonio, she moved to New York to live in the Barbizon Hotel for Women (an East Coast version of the Hollywood Studio Club where Farrah stayed her first few months there) and try ballet. She wound up instead in commercials, first with Listerine and then as one of the country's most highly paid models. When Jaclyn switched from Breck to Wella Balsam, she got a part originally written for Farrah. (Both Angels pitch separate products for Wella.)

Some people say that Jaclyn is even prettier than Farrah. A brunette with green eyes, Jaclyn measures up to the sensitive character she plays— sans the hustling. In fact, it was she who rejected the Las Vegas gloss to her role but agreed to go along with the hard-life background. "There is a certain vulnerability about Jackie," one producer says, "that makes you believe that she is an orphan in the show."

Leading the Angels is . . .

Sabrina Duncan
(Kate Jackson)

Sabrina looks like an angel, and is. Tall, lean of limb, with a today sense of humor, her glance is level, her manner clear-headed. An "army brat," educated in Europe where she grew up around military bases, she speaks five languages fluently and is bright enough to match wits with any adversary. There is imagination in everything she does. And she has that rare ability to be good at anything she tries.

Sabrina can disarm a heavy with her charm or a skilled karate chop. Of the three Angels, she would be considered the intellect (though they are all bright women of today), and the more pragmatic and coolly analytical of the trio in the face of danger (which is often). She's the Angels' unofficial leader. The one who would be the calm in the eye of a storm and make the final decision if there was conflict among the three.

A private person off the job, Sabrina lives in a high-rise security building. While available for dates with eligible males (her standards are high), there is only one special man in her life: her ex-husband, a plainclothes detective on the L.A.P.D. They went through the Academy together, fell in love, got married, found that two cops in the same household didn't work; but their relationship now is better than it's ever been. When questioned by the other Angels as to why she and her ex don't remarry, Sabrina's answer is the inevitable: "Why spoil a good thing?"

The most outspoken of the girls on the set, Kate is usually given the expository parts in the show. She is also the most experienced of the troop, having played, among other parts, nurse Danko on "The Rookies" before signing on as an Angel. In fact, the series sprang in part from her brow. Her producers wanted a show about "three karate-chopping types," she remembers. "I said, suppose they work for a detective named ... Harry. He calls them on a squawk box ... Then I saw a picture on the wall of three angels ..."

The daughter of a building materials wholesaler in Birmingham, Alabama, Kate wanted from childhood to be an actress. After studying at Birmingham-Southern University, she did summer stock in Vermont and made the soaps in ABC's "Dark Shadows." The result was a four-year stint in "The Rookies," where she spent days off studying directing and editing techniques.

Like Farrah she is a natural athlete and once considered pro tennis as a career. She still works out weekends with a coach. Though Kate once lived with actor Edward Albert, Jr., she told *People*: "My love life ain't what it used to be. I've stopped smoking and drinking and staying out late. I've got to discipline myself or the work would kill me."

By virtue of her experience as an actress working in television shows rather than commercials, Kate is paid $10,000 per show, twice as much as Farrah and Jackie, who get, $5,000 apiece. But her overall take is piddling compared to Farrah and Jackie, whose bank accounts are bulging with fees from commercials. Each earns well over $100,000 annually from peddling products. Kate still receives residuals from "The Rookies." Home for her is not a mansion, but a hi-rise apartment to which she fled after a burglary in her house.

Since Charlie, whose voice belongs to actor John Forsthye, is never seen, he must have a physical go-between. Forsythe refused to appear unless his face was shown on the screen. His voice was perfect, and network officials agreed to use his sound effects while hiring another actor willing to expose the back of his head and occasionally a forearm. Keeping in touch with Charlie while bolstering—or inadvertently botching up—the Angels is . . .

John Bosley
(David Doyle)

Bosley is fiftyish, cheerful, round-faced, with a dryly devastating sense of humor. He's the middleman between Charlie and the Angels, is their contact in each episode, and should be used whenever needed—but never in a situation one of the Angels can handle themselves, or in a situation that would overshadow any of the girls dramatically.

Somewhat of a bumbler, Bosley might occasionally (but inadvertently) blow a cover, a clue, etc., to cause the Angels further danger on a case.

And, no matter what, Bosley always wants to ingratiate himself with the Boss, Charlie.

Warding off charges that the Angels are being "exploited" on the series, Jaclyn Smith recently told the Dallas *Times Herald*: "I don't feel that's true at all. This show has to be more than three pretty faces flitting around. The way I see it is that we are three very different types who happen to blend together well. Nobody claims that the show is intellectual. It's just a fun thing, and people apparently want light entertainment at night."

The Angels work hard for their money. They soar above the material of the show which has been billed by some critics as prime-time girlie fare. Though "Charlie's Angels" has received the highest Nielsen ratings, its intelligence quotient is said to be at the comic book level of, say, "Batman." Commenting on the show's content, an ABC spokesman says, "It's just entertainment. Why fix it, change it? There are three beautiful girls and that's what counts. Other than that, who cares?"

The Angels do, for sure. Even for such on-the-go girls, their schedule is arduous. Each script is fifty-six pages long, and sometimes the girls don't get them until the night before shooting. They must be ready to recite eight pages of script a day. There are no days devoted to rehearsals—directors merely move the girls around like furniture on the set. Nonetheless there is only so far that they can go in arranging the Angels, who have on occasion been unbudgeable. Like the time Jackie Smith refused to lure a strange man back to her place or Farrah refused to parade around in a bikini when the scene did not call for it. One episode, particularly well received by viewers, "Angels in Chains," was a less-than-subtle play on sado-masochistic chic. The plot involved the three purposely getting themselves jailed at the Pine Parish Prison in search of a young female prisoner for a client. There a sadistic woman guard commands, "Okay, girls, strip down to your birthday suits," and while they shower, she leers at them. A mandatory post-shower rap calls for the Angels to open their towels and be sprayed with disinfectant. After Jill (Farrah) protests that she's roughed up slightly, the female guard tells the warden: "I'll try not to bruise her tender skin too much." Later the girls are given a choice: work in the potato fields or join the jail's own whorehouse. In later shows the Angels, at their urging, were given more say in the roles they would play.

When Rosenzweig came in as a third producer, his heightened consciousness resulted in more autonomy for the Angels. For one thing, he invested more power in them, devising ways for them to crack the case as opposed to relying on Charlie for instruction. Secondly, by placing more emphasis on character than plot development, he allowed them to be more well-defined characters. "The show has a great appeal to women," he explains, "because of the buddy system. There are three dynamite ladies in charge, and they like each other. Their relationship does not grow out of the traditional male view of women. They're also every bit as competitive in their work as 'Starsky and Hutch.' The Angels are unique in that they don't need help." Even "Policewoman" (Angie Dickinson), as successful as it is, relies on the traditional male-female relationship by having her consult the boss regularly.

In their working lives, the girls show a superhuman energy. "I don't know how anybody does it," says Rosenzweig. Except for weekends off, they work seven days straight for each show—Monday, Tuesday, Wednesday, Thursday, Friday, Monday, and Tuesday . . . and then they start the next day, Wednesday, on another show and finish that up the next Thursday, only to begin again. Each weekly show, which comprises some forty-six minutes of screentime, after commercials, takes seven days to complete.

Though union laws restrict actors and actresses from working without a twelve-hour grace period between shooting, that does *not* include the time devoted to makeup and hair. Assuming the Angels finish shooting at 8:00 P.M., they are not required to show up until 8:00 A.M., the customary hour to begin filming. Realistically, this is not possible because time is needed to prepare their faces—and hair—for the show.

When male actors stroll on the set at 8:00 A.M., the girls have already been there an hour-and-a-half. Their day begins with skilled application of facial tone coloring and eyeshadow by the company's two makeup men. The process takes about forty minutes for each girl. Farrah's appearance calls for beige colors that flatter her face and golden complexion. Though the production's two professional hairstylists are at the girls' side the entire shooting day, Farrah and Jackie, of hair commercials fame, prefer to comb out their own locks.

"Everybody pictures a movie star's schedule as something utterly wonderful," Farrah laughs. "Breakfast in bed and maybe somebody doing my nails while I sleep."

A more realistic picture is a typical working day in the life of Farrah; she is picked up by a limousine at 5:30 A.M. which takes her to either Sound Stage Eight at Twentieth Century-Fox or various locations around the Los Angeles area. In addition to the makeup and the hair sets, wardrobes—sometimes as many as five dresses for one segment—are laid out for her. By filming time she has already put in an hour-and-a-half on the job.

Depending on whether they film at Twentieth Century, still dotted with Western-style sets, or outside locations, Farrah's cut-off time varies. On the lot she has a 7:00 P.M. cut-off clause in her contract allowing her to attend to her equally important home life. Farrah has Lee waiting for supper. Jackie is divorced, and Kate is single. But Farrah is lucky to hit the road for home before 8:00 P.M., because first she must take off her makeup, change her clothes, and inspect the next day's wardrobe.

About four days of each show are done on the lot, and one of them is devoted to wardrobe. "No matter how exhausted Farrah may be," a producer reports, "she bubbles over when she is trying on clothes. She comes alive, like a gleeful child." Such an exercise may keep Farrah on the set until after 10:00 P.M. "Once I heard Farrah talking to Lee," Rosenzweig reports. "She was late in wardrobe and called, to discover that he had fallen asleep. She was genuinely upset, 'Lee, please wait . . . I have the meal all set and want to cook it for you. Oh, I never do anything right!' "

Her taste in clothes is superb. Though wardrobe people are hired, in part, to select clothes for the girls, Farrah prefers to do her own shopping. Usually she reserves part of her weekend, when not filming a commercial or competing on the tennis court, to this pursuit. Once Farrah puts together a wardrobe, she leaves a card, saying that the studio will pick it up. She is allowed to keep whatever she likes for her personal use. Says Barney Rosenzweig: "Farrah has style. Once I was around when she was picking an evening gown for one scene. The first was $85, the second $175, and the third $1,200. In this instance her wardrobe people had brought the dresses to her. She asked which one I liked, and I said they all looked beautiful. Farrah picked the $85 gown, and she looked smashing in it—she was right!"

Sometimes Farrah's fantastic taste runs into what some network executives might call "more than lavish." The wardrobe budget per show is $4,000. On one occasion a store called to say, "We have

Farrah Fawcett-Majors here, and she wants to buy $200 worth of scarves." The girl who somehow always gets her way did it again. Another time when Farrah was asked to do a spot on "The Captain and Tennille" to hike up the ABC show's sagging ratings, she agreed, but not for $5,000. "I saw the most beautiful coat," she told the executive. "It's a little more than $5,000 though." The price tag was $7,500, and ABC agreed to it. But two hours later, Farrah's agent called to say that Farrah had been mistaken about the cost—it was really $9,500. By then, Jackie and Kate had agreed to their terms so Farrah's timing was luckily perfect. In short, network officials, through clenched teeth, bit the bullet and financed the fur coat.

"Underneath it all," Rosenzweig says, "Farrah is the iron butterfly. She has the sensuality that appeals to every guy and the little girl about her that brings out the paternal instinct."

After one filming session, Farrah, exhausted and minus ten pounds, broke down in tears. The pressure had gotten to her—and this was understandable. Angels, too, are mere mortals though their hours might indicate otherwise. On the three days that they film outside the lot, at different locations around the city, Farrah does not have the protection of a cut-off clause. The reason is that shooting is too costly to break. In some instances, the girls and all the equipment and props have been hauled as far as forty miles away. It is not unusual to break close to midnight on these locations. All together this can mean almost an eighteen-hour day.

A normal day runs about fourteen hours, at the Fox lot, located in West Los Angeles. Whereas the studio once had seemingly endless acres of space to create different settings, today much of the backlot is now Century City, a futuristic complex of hi-rise residential, commercial, and shopping centers. But wherever the Angels have to tread, their $25,000 Pace Arrow trailers follow them. On the set, each retreats to her own abode, stocked with flowers and Perrier water, to change or just relax between takes. Both Jackie and Farrah have color TV sets, but the more intellectual Kate opted for book-shelves.

"I can't even take a snooze," Farrah says. On one Los Angeles location, a public park, hordes of teen-age boys jumped on top of her trailer and shouted obscenities at her. Sometimes more subtle older men will find out the name of someone close to Farrah and put in an emergency call to the studio. A once frantic Farrah, using the expertise gained as one of "Charlie's Angels," figured out the nature of these kinds of bogus calls, and thus has learned to ignore them.

On the set, Farrah has a reputation among the men, already seduced by her beauty, for being smart. Sweet and considerate, Farrah can also be firm with fans. "She can really get angry when they crowd in on her," he adds.

Allen Baron, a sensitive, reflective man who directed Farrah in two shows of "Charlie's Angels," remembers his first meeting with her: "Initially I thought this is just another model with a lot of hair and white teeth and probably no talent. Then when I was working with her, I saw a charming, sweet, disarming quality—not unlike Marilyn Monroe. I saw a certain innocence."

With some one hundred TV shows including

"Switch" and "Barney Miller" to his directing credit, Allen Baron is a Hollywood fixture and was once a neighbor of Marilyn Monroe. Once Allen and Marilyn talked late into the night. "I don't see Farrah as a great dramatic actress, but as an appealing personality," he continues. "The difference between Farrah and Marilyn Monroe is that Marilyn had a self-destructive impulse, doubted herself, and had a generally poor self-image. This girl has a healthy one, pro-life."

Proof of this positive quality is her ingrained, instinctive sense of humor. "If something amuses Farrah," he says, "her response is full and childlike. She'll giggle. It's not as though she thinks 'How should I react?'. She just does."

Producer Rosenzweig goes a step further: "Farrah is an authentically talented comedienne. She just bubbles. She is probably not as pretty as the other two girls. But all together what she does with herself physically makes her the most attractive."

Underlying this sense of humor, he says, is "a great sense of her own feet of clay." Rosenzweig's résumé ironically has a huge caricature of himself bearded and with a tennis racket in hand, with the footprints of such stars as Robert Redford and Paul Newman under his own sneakers. He looks like the Malibu version of Ozymandias. "Farrah is not afraid to wear a funny costume," he adds. "She always soars above the material."

Farrah's special gift for comedy, however, does not preclude her from taking more serious roles. "She always wanted a dramatic part," Rosenzweig recalls. "One episode, written for Kate, was given to Farrah after Farrah asked for a more sophisticated, serious part." A policy on the show, according to Rosenzweig, was to give each girl a shot at the most demanding parts so they would have something to show at the end of the season.

In this instance the show was "Jericho," the story of a professional assassin with a list of people he plans to kill. It is Jill's (Farrah's) job to befriend the assassin, played by Fernando Lamas, a suave actor in his fifties. The idea was that one of them would be close to him when he made his move. "We felt Kate would be more believable, convincing, in a sophisticated low-cut gown," Rosenzweig recalls, "but when we decided to give Farrah the part, she was excellent. She was bright and sophisticated as she gave him a tour of Los Angeles. It became clear that there was no reason why Farrah shouldn't get any part."

Director Baron adds to this: "There's a determination in Farrah with regard to life and career that seems to be fairly well defined." He attributes her growth as an actress to a combination of being interested in taking direction and yet using her discretion. "She was very eager to learn and listen, grateful for ideas and suggestions, and she responded," he recalls. "At the same time, if there was something she did not like, she would speak up."

A rare moment that captures a certain subtlety about Farrah flashes across his mind, and director Allen Baron remembers aloud: "An assistant director was urging her on the set in a way she did not like. It was like a buzzing in her ear. She looked at him as if to say, 'Don't impose on my area,' and almost in a whisper said, 'That's enough'." It was not a matter of some egocentric star pulling rank. "I felt Farrah was strong enough to catch his eye and assert herself in a quiet way. Other stars I have known might have been more hostile, violent. Not Farrah—though she is very capable of being very determined."

He elaborates on the contradiction that is Farrah Fawcett-Majors. The devout Catholic who was willing to participate in a trial living arrangement for two years before marrying Lee. The woman who looks elegant and sophisticated in evening clothes and also loves to run free on the beach. "The gamut—the childlike nature and the determination—is what makes her interesting," Baron says. "That she has all these qualities within her. One is not untrue to the other, of course."

Baron, twenty years in the business, says that he has never been deluged by so many people wanting to go on the "Charlie" set. "They're responding to more than the hair and the white teeth—the intuitive sense of self that makes her so interesting. That wonderful interior that is intuitive rather than intellectual. She is a cross between Judy Holliday and Marilyn Monroe with a potentially great mass appeal."

In a show known for its daring hijinks and acrobatics, Farrah gets high marks from her stuntwoman double, Glynn Rubin. She is close to Farrah's size and height and, as a blonde, does not need a wig, which tends to look artificial and somewhat unwieldy. "Farrah is delightful to work with," she says. "She's very professional, which counts for so much in my business. She never keeps people waiting on the set. She does what she can to aid me. If I have to take a fall, Farrah will wear long sleeves so I can get away with elbow pads during the rescue. Anything Farrah can do to make the job safer or easier she'll do."

Before Glynn's arrival on the set, Farrah had been slammed to the ground by a careening car. "Farrah doesn't take any unnecessary chances," Glynn says. "In fact during my stunt, when I jumped out of the window of a speeding truck, I think I scared her to death. She said, " 'Terrific' to me."

Glynn Rubin, who has performed similar feats in the movie *The Duchess and the Dirt Water Fox* and "Starsky and Hutch," says that Farrah's athleticism is a bonus for her. "It means more work, more fun, for me," she says. Another plus is that Farrah walks a fine line between what she can and wants to do and what the producers will allow on the show. Obvious stunts like speeding on a skateboard, or jumping out of speeding vehicles, automatically go to stuntwoman Rubin. "Farrah is experienced and bright enough to know what is involved," Glynn Rubin explains. "A lot of younger stars think that they're chicken if they don't do it. This is the wrong—and a dangerous—attitude."

Stunt coordinator Dick Ziker praises Farrah as one of the most athletic actresses around. "She keeps herself in incredible shape," he says. "Farrah has an incredible bounce to her step. I call her 'the little bunny rabbit'."

Fans, producers, and directors alike view Farrah as a sexy, spunky superstar. They feel the sky is the limit for her.

As an Angel, Farrah will not be grounded for too much longer as Charlie's sexiest sleuth. Maybe this will have been the last season. Or perhaps she may remain in the series for another season. The unfettered, yet disciplined Farrah Fawcett-Majors, with the counsel of her husband Lee, will make that decision.

"When Farrah said she might not do the show she was not angling for money," director Allen Baron theorizes, "but to have more time for the joy of living. I admire this attitude—as opposed to people who can't give up the money for fear of being broke. Farrah opted for more free time. Her *joie de vivre* exceeds her greed."

If the past is a compass to her future direction, success is surely in Farrah's path . . . .

Chapter 7

Farrah at Play

"The worst thing pressure could do to me would be to make me say, 'That's it!' and split. I can walk away from it."

Thus speaks Farrah Fawcett-Majors, a girl with a natural talent for work and play. The sparkling quality that she brings to her role as one of "Charlie's Angels" is easily transferable to her private life. This is no superstar smiling on the screen and sulking in her living room! "Farrah has a very strong personality and a positive attitude toward life," says Cathy Amsterdam, her personal secretary. "I'm not sure her ambition is specific. No matter what she does, she does well."

As hard as Farrah works, she does not have to put the brakes on herself to relax and have fun. Always she is in control of her drive instead of allowing ambition to rule her. According to friends, Farrah is an enormously well-integrated person and thus capable of making a clear and healthy division between her career and her personal life. Almost never paralyzed by indecision, Farrah manages her days so that they are both full and productive. Though Farrah knows when to wind down from work, she would never bow to exhaustion if there is a job to be completed. Her energies are well used in the pursuit of goals and pleasure.

Part of Farrah's magic is that she does not play-act through her life. Unlike other superstars who never know whether they are "on" or "off," Farrah likes just plain being herself. She knows who she is and does not have to be paged six times at the Polo Lounge at the Beverly Hills Hotel to gain an identity. Instead of lying poolside and tilting her face to the sun to absorb its every last ray, Farrah keeps her golden look by running on the beach and playing a competitive game of tennis. There is an evenness about her tan and also her life.

Evenings are equally unstaged. Rarely dressing up, Farrah prefers pants, blouses, and sweaters that match such interests as a game of poker, visiting friends at a nearby home, or taking in an occasional movie. Often after a dinner at Chasen's, the star-studded restaurant, or Matteo's, particularly good Italian fare, or the Palm, for steaks and lobster, Farrah will retire for the night. She likes to run around on a tennis court instead of to disclotheques. Fun for Farrah does not require standard Hollywood props like pot and cocaine. Other superstars may awaken like zombies the next noon, but by that hour Farrah has probably played a few sets of tennis.

Understandably, Farrah shrugs off the inevitable comparison of herself to Marilyn Monroe, her predecessor as America's sex symbol. In a recent interview with *McCall's* magazine, Farrah declared that she had no intention of becoming another Marilyn Monroe, whom she described as probably "insecure" and added, "I'm not like her at all."

While casual shots of Farrah abound, most photographs of Marilyn were somewhat contrived. Marilyn Monroe's essential look was man-made—the walk, the hair, the coy voice and the sultry look. "Farrah can wash her hair and then stick it in a hat or leave it frizzy," a friend says admiringly. "She couldn't care less if she has to run around town. She doesn't worry if her hair is droopy. She'll take a tennis lesson in the middle of the day. Farrah is not primping." Even Norma Jean's name, Marilyn Monroe, was a Hollywood creation. Farrah Fawcett, of course, is her real name! Rarely rising before noon when she was not working, Marilyn Monroe spent the better part of her initial waking moments just preparing herself to deal with the day ahead. Unlike Farrah, who remains close with her parents today, Marilyn as a child was shuttled between foster homes. By the time Marilyn Monroe was Farrah's age, thirty, she had been married three times—at seventeen to policeman James Doherty; then baseball star Joe DiMaggio; and later playwright Arthur Miller who wrote the movie *The Misfits* for Marilyn. At the age of thirty-six, Marilyn Monroe overdosed on sleeping pills, and her only friend beside her was the telephone on which she had fallen.

At thirty, Farrah's life as a superstar has just begun. It is only in the last year that she has emerged as the all-American phenomenon—all the more remarkable since she is a TV star and not as yet a movie actress. In recent years cults have grown up around such television stars as The Fonz (Henry Winkler) and Mary Tyler Moore, for example, but no one has captured the adoration of the public as has Farrah Fawcett-Majors.

Farrah's style of play relaxation underlines even more the distinction between herself and Marilyn Monroe. During Marilyn's heyday, stars would flock in the late evening to such clubs as The Cloisters, The Crescendo, Moulin Rouge, The Slate Brothers, and Ciro's. There comedians like Buddy Hackett, Don Rickles, and Mort Sahl played to full houses and generally tipsy crowds. And at P.J., another favorite habitat, Trini Lopez was discovered by Frank Sinatra. Gossip columnists would get a glimpse of the goings-on and dutifully report it in the next day's newspaper. Marilyn Monroe was sighted on more than a few occasions. And her rumored romances were also cited in the aforementioned pieces. Today most of these places have shut down—and with them, out went the mink stoles and cocktail dresses.

Perhaps more than any superstar in history, Farrah Fawcett-Majors evokes a joy and spontaneity about living instead of melancholia, depression, and the staleness of staying up half the night in a smoke-filled club. Farrah embodies the casual, clean-living, outdoorsy life. She is a delightful combination of the new woman playing sports and the old-fashioned girl baking cookies. In a city like Los Angeles, where people display their credit card possessions around their necks, on their fingers, and in their choice of cars, Farrah has more cash than flash. There is nothing flamboyant about her handling of material possessions, which include a Mercedes hooked up with a phone to her husband's twin auto.

Merry-go-round marriages and musical chairs affairs do not interest her. She remains married to the man, actor Lee Majors, whom she met shortly after arriving in Hollywood almost nine years ago. While they appreciate the public's worship, both Farrah and Lee value most the deep affection they have for each other.

Their closest friends are Bernie Gelson, fifty-seven, the owner of a chain of high priced specialty supermarkets in the Los Angeles area, and his wife, Ann, thirty-six, whom Farrah met when she came to Hollywood. "They're a terrific couple," says Gelson, "and two of the nicest people you'll ever meet. We go to their home or they come to ours. They're like anybody else except for their work." Gelson met Lee for the first time at Farrah's Wedding, and the two couples have been extremely close ever since.

Weekends, Farrah and Lee usually play mixed doubles with Bernie and Ann Gelson at the latter's Chatsworth ranch about twenty minutes from Los Angeles. The Gelsons have a tennis court by a lake populated with ducks and wild geese. Lee keeps his Arabian horse there. Often they will be joined by comic Dick Van Patten, his wife, Pat, and their two sons for round-robin matches. "Farrah plays with the boys to improve her game," Gelson says. "She's a strong player and hits hard enough to keep up a good rally with them. The Van Patten sons are tremendous tennis players. One is a teaching pro, and the other a top-ranked amateur who is the best player in Hollywood."

Around the Gelson ranch Farrah enjoys spending time with the couple's two children, seven-year-old Joe and nine-year-old Jessica. "Sometimes other children will be playing at the house and see Farrah and Lee," Gelson says, "and this is a real treat for them. But we would never invite people over to meet them. They are always mobbed by fans. Sometimes it can be frightening—it seems as though hundreds of people are closing in on you. Farrah and Lee really like their privacy."

Farrah likes to sit down with Jessica Gelson and draw with her. "Farrah is a greatly talented artist," says Gelson. "She could have made a fine living in this field. You should see the work she has done. There are some magnificent sculptures in her house."

One evening during the week the two couples may dine at Bistro, a chic French restaurant or, for Chinese food, at Mr. Chow's in Beverly Hills. They turn in early. "Farrah and Lee have very early calls," says Gelson, "so we never stay out late. By ten at night Farrah and Lee have already shut off their phones." On days that Farrah is working, but has a later call than usual—after 8:00 A.M.—she will ring up Ann Gelson for tennis singles. Sometimes Farrah may sneak in a set during the afternoon. Rain never deters them—they rent an indoor court.

The two couples visit New York City together. If they spend three days there, they will attend at least three Broadway shows. Their favorite dining places are the posh Grenouille and "21." "Lee and Farrah wrote their names in the wine cellar at '21'," Gelson recalls. Two favorite plays they all saw were: *Same Time Next Year* and *A Chorus Line*.

Lee and Farrah favor both the Regency Hotel, on Park Avenue in the Sixties, and the Park Lane on Central Park South. Both hotels are frequented by the rich and famous from all over the world. More modern than landmarks like the Waldorf-Astoria and the Plaza, these hotels tend to have huge rooms. The Park Lane, just down the block from the Plaza Hotel, offers panoramic views of Central Park. "Lee and Farrah like to have a view of the park," says Gelson. "They like to look out at the ice-skating rink." It was at the Wollman ice-skating rink that scenes from Erich Segal's *Love Story* were filmed. In summer the greenery of the area appeals to Lee and Farrah. With the hansom cabs lined up at the curb, they can have the illusion that they are in the country. And yet the theaters and museums are nearby for them.

"Farrah is a phenomenon," Gelson says with the greatest respect and admiration. "She is the most down-to-earth person I've ever met. She is just a charmer. She is wonderful!" If the two couples do not want to dine out, they may all get together at either of their homes for a meal.

Around her home Farrah likes to cook when she is not too busy shooting the series. She particularly relishes the idea of making Lee supper. Farrah also likes to bake. Her specialties are southern-style: chocolate chip cookies, cornbread, and chili. Farrah is also something of a muncher between meals, and she eats Cheetos, Fritos, and drinks Coca-Cola or diet versions of it. But behind every bite or sip is an ingrained self-discipline. "Everybody will eat one chocolate chip cookie after another," one friend says. "Farrah will eat half of one."

She balances her junk food binges with a steady diet of exercise at work and play. Farrah jumps rope for ten minutes every morning and every night and also does calisthenics. "She takes very good care of her body," the friend says. "That IN-CREDIBLE body!" As often as possible, Farrah treats herself to a sauna and jacuzzi.

All of the above pays off for someone who likes to shop as much as Farrah. A favorite store is Charles Gallay in Beverly Hills. Located on Camden Drive, with Madison Avenue-like boutiques, it is a block from Rodeo, the Fifth Avenue of Los Angeles. The place has a style all its own. The front of the building is in black marble, and the inside has an apothecary-like cash register. The clothing has a vibrant, multicolored sporty look. Leather bags and dishrag scarves, which are used as either scarves or purses, decorate the floor. One of Farrah's favorite designers, twenty-seven-year-old J. C. de Castelbajac, a Frenchman, is well represented here. His knit polos with painted designs of sailboats look particularly good on Farrah, who this season may be sporting his linen-weave Bermuda shorts, with Ivy League buckles on the back.

Closer to her Bel Air home, in the San Fernando Valley area, are Country Club Fashions and Pickwick, both located in the spiffy Sherman Oaks "Fashion Square." At Country Club, fashion coordinator Rosalie Blackstone says that Farrah is a Saturday regular when she is not working. Sometimes

Farrah's wardrobe people or secretary, she says, will collect outfits for Farrah. "Farrah used to enjoy shopping a lot more when she wasn't so busy," says Ms. Blackstone.

Ms. Blackstone, a kindly woman who has handled many celebrities, says Farrah has been shopping there for at least the last six years. "Farrah buys a little bit of everything," she says. "She knows what she wants." Though Farrah's definite taste allows her to whisk through the store, she is, according to Ms. Blackstone, a woman who regards shopping as an amusement rather than a chore.

"Farrah is the sweetest person I have ever worked with," Ms. Blackstone continues. "She is always so polite. She says, 'Thank you,' or 'No, thank you' all the time." More often than not, it's 'thank you,' for with Farrah's perfect figure everything looks great on her. New Hero pants, in all colors, Sonia Rykiel tunic tops and sweaters. New Men French cotton jeans, in orange, white, blue, peach. Rafael suits, Dorothee Bis sweaters. "Farrah used to buy a lot more evening dresses," Ms. Blackstone says, "but now she's a jersey girl, very casual." Country Club Fashions, a high-priced store with many French imports, sells the Theodore label, another Farrah favorite, which is designed by the owner's wife.

Often when Farrah's mother is visiting, the two of them will spend a Saturday afternoon in the store. "Mrs. Fawcett is a very attractive woman," says fashion coordinator Blackstone. "They really enjoy themselves in here. You can tell that they are a very, very close family."

Across the way from Country Club Fashions is Pickwick, and Farrah and her mother stop in there too. The Hungarian-born manager is as charming and helpful as a sweet southern belle. A chic store, it also houses French imports like Cacharel shirts, Dorothee Bis, French wool gabardine pants, which are part of Farrah's wardrobe. But the All-American girl also likes California designers like Norman Todd.

When Farrah's mother visits, she usually stays two or three months at a time. Another favorite pastime of this mother and daughter is cleaning out the closets and, of course, stocking them with the latest fashions. "Farrah really likes having her parents stay with her," one friend says. "She likes having their companionship." The Fawcetts usually show up about every four months or so. Her mother also helps Farrah work on the house, which is faultlessly decorated in French Provincial style.

The Farrah Fawcett-Majors family also includes a mini-menagerie with such dogs as a German shepherd and a Pekingese. Farrah gave her Yorkie mutt, Cammy, to her mother. About the only instance of tension between the Angels was after a part was written into one of the scripts for a dog. Jaclyn Smith showed up with her poodle, Albert, and soon Kate brought along her husky, Catcher. Before long, Farrah appeared with a Pekingese called Pansie. The cameo part, which each Angel secretly hoped would go to her dog, was ultimately struck from the script. Farrah has also brought her black Afghan, Satchel, to work and hoped for cameos in which Satchel might save her life.

Farrah does not read a great deal. She is of the TV generation. On the set, Kate Jackson, the most bookish of the trio, would give Farrah a book and try to make her read it. One time she brought Farrah *Catcher in the Rye* and said, "I know you'll never read it. But it's a wonderful book."

Her reading tastes run to Gothic and romantic novels like Rosemary Rogers' *Sweet Savage Love*. "Usually Marge Schicktanz [Farrah's commercial agent] will bring the books and leave them with Farrah," the friend says. "That's what Farrah will read." Currently Lee and Farrah, who recently formed a production company, have been trying to buy the movie rights to make and star in a picture based on *Sweet Savage Love*.

When Lee is out of town, Farrah will go to the movies with Marge Schicktanz. Farrah raved about *A Star Is Born*, featuring Barbra Streisand, who, with her former hairstylist and now steady companion Jon Peters, produced the film. "Farrah is very private," a friend says. "She did not indicate whether or not she identified with the movie. But I know she thought about the film quite some time after seeing it."

Farrah and Lee are devoted to each other's needs. If one of them is tired, the other may go out alone with friends. Lee, by nature something of a loner, occasionally dines by himself. Farrah once in a while has played poker and gone to Santa Anita racetrack with friends.

On one occasion, Texas sculptor Charles Umlauf recalls, Lee wanted to watch the football game while Farrah was eager to attend an exhibit of her former professor. "I called up and Lee said Farrah was not feeling well," Umlauf recalls. "When I spoke to Farrah later, she explained that Lee wanted to watch the football game instead of going to the exhibit. Farrah went by herself."

In the last year Farrah bowed out of celebrity sporting events because of the pressures on Lee to make a bionic performance. Another reason was that just getting through the crowds that swarm around Farrah, like honey bees around a flower, would be a major athletic triumph. However, these two active stars may be resuming their participation in such events. In April, Farrah and Lee played in the Dinah Shore Celebrity Challenge of the Sexes at the Mission Hills Country Club in Palm Springs, California. Dinah, a good friend, likes to golf with Farrah.

Often Farrah cannot commit herself to events more than two weeks in advance. "Her schedule is so demanding that she tends not to make plans too far ahead," says personal secretary Cathy Amsterdam. Cathy, daughter of comedian Morey Amsterdam and herself an attractive, wholesome blonde with beautiful blue eyes, came to work for Farrah after deciding between that job and work at a drug rehabilitation center.

Still, Farrah appears to be in full control of her play-time. An early riser, she apportions her time in order to fit the things she gets pleasure doing into her tight filming schedule. Her career and personal life are so well sorted out that she is never faced with the sorrowful perception that the day has come and gone, passed her by.

"Farrah has such a strong sense of self," says

Cathy Amsterdam, "that she always gets good results without going on a pilgrimage of the self."

Whether it is on the set or the tennis court, Farrah always comes out on top!

Chapter 8

Farrah's Philosophy

The gentle curve of the Santa Monica Mountains winds slowly down to the sea through the western part of Los Angeles. Before the hills meet the water as craggy bluffs, the rolling canyons of the mountains are sharply etched through the chic suburb of Bel Air.

It was here, in this wilderness and natural surrounding, that Farrah Fawcett took Lee Majors for her husband. The setting was not the tinny and plastic wedding chapels of Las Vegas, but the idyllic and wild—even savage in nature—setting of the Hotel Bel Air with its swan-filled lake and arbors overflowing with shrubs and flowers.

Farrah looked radiant and fresh in an ivory silk peasant dress smocked at the sleeves and the waist. The dress, designed by Theadora van Runkle, had tiny seed pearls in the smocking. Over her lustrous hair Farrah wore a big picture hat, as in the portraits of the eighteenth-century English painter Joshua Reynolds. Lee was handsomely groomed in a white linen suit that Rhett Butler might have sported in *Gone with the Wind*. Together Farrah and Lee struck a pose of grace and beauty of bygone days.

The setting reflected Farrah's life and philosophy. Gentle, clean living is her trademark. The outdoors is the backdrop of her life. At the heart of her existence is a loving marriage and a strong feeling for family. Her sense of self is rooted in the soil of the land and the decent, honest values indigenous to it.

The premise of her life grows out of beliefs that she has acted on since childhood. With Farrah, it is certainly not a matter of inventing a hypothesis for living and then fitting the events into the formula. At the same time she does not latch on to clichés or experiment with newfangled, shabby adventures.

Perhaps the one absolute of her life is treating other people carefully and politely. "If Kate is sad," Farrah told *People* in a cover story about the Angels, "then I am sad too." Comedian Carl Reiner describes a Farrah temper tantrum: "She told me she was mad at her maid, but knew how to get even. She said, 'I'm not going to fix her hair any more!'"

While other people may go through a dozen motions to achieve a certain end, it usually takes Farrah half the effort. She does not linger over successes or disappointments, of which she has had very few, but just moves on to the next thing at hand. And making a decision does not require a summit conference for her. Bolstered by a strong

Catholic upbringing, Farrah rarely goes through moral dilemmas that could consume enormous energy. Simply, Farrah knows her own mind and which course of action would be appropriate to her style of living.

Friends are convinced that Farrah was born under a lucky star because magical things always seem to happen to her. What she sees is what she gets! Farrah has a strong gift of intuition, they say, and relies on it in a calm and unstudied manner. Rather than trying to make things happen in her life, Farrah willingly and joyfully accepts the good things that may come her way. Later she does not question the how and why of it or torment herself with guilt over such good fortune.

Farrah, of course, does not rest on her laurels. Once she becomes the recipient of a good turn she positions herself in such a way as to make the most of it. For example, once she emerged as the most beloved of the Angels, she posed for a poster that is now reaping her even greater financial reward. And so is the Farrah Fawcett-Majors doll fashioned after her gorgeous look.

"Farrah takes life with a grain of salt and a sense of humor," says Cathy Amsterdam. "Nothing is really that serious. For the moment, yes—but not after that."

Nowhere is this attitude more apparent than in the way Farrah thinks about beauty. Once asked by a reporter if she could recall the moment when she discovered how beautiful she is, Farrah replied, "Just a few seconds ago—after the makeup man got through."

Hugh York, the hair stylist who created the Farrah Fawcett-Majors look, considers her to be one of the most beautiful women in the world. He says that Farrah is aware of her beauty, but she is not fixated on it. Proof of this, he says, is how Farrah reacted to his jokingly saying, "Oh, you're so beautiful, Farrah. Now if you only had a few more teeth, you could race at Hialeah." Instead of galloping off to the oral surgeon, Farrah giggled, all the while flashing a mouth overflowing with gleaming white teeth.

"I've seen Farrah for twelve hours at a time on the set," says Cathy Amsterdam, "and over and over again I thought to myself, 'This woman is so beautiful.'"

Yet Farrah herself does not believe that she is flawless. "My arms are too bony," she has complained to disbelieving friends. "My teeth are too large." She is generous with compliments about the way other people look. "She says Cher is prettier than herself," one friend mentioned.

Unlike many other fantastic-looking people, Farrah does not assign all that much value to physical appearance. While she never judges people by the way they look, Farrah does put emphasis on the body. "But this is more in terms of being healthy and fit," a friend says.

Farrah herself is skeptical about what beauty can mean in a person's life. While she appreciates the compliments, Farrah cautions: "Very good-looking people can easily fall into a trap that's hard to get out of. Being considered nothing but a mannequin is not only frustrating, it can hurt. I've got plenty of brains and what I hope is talent, so I sometimes resent it when I'm described in terms of my exterior self. That's especially true when you're a model or do ads for grooming products."

Then in typical Farrah fashion, she adds, "People may say I'm a sex symbol, but I tell them I'm simply an everyday woman. I really am."

What does this "everyday woman" think about marriage, stardom, money, the future? Here is some Farrah Fawcett-Majors philosophy. Farrah is not a self-appointed philosopher who likes to make grandiose statements about the world. She does not go in for highfalutin' philosophies, theories, or prescriptions for living. Farrah has expressed some thoughts and feelings, but almost always in response to journalists' inquiries.

Marriage

Marriage is the core of Farrah's existence. Her relationship with Lee takes precedence over every other facet of her life. It is what gives her the most meaning, comfort, and pleasure.

Friends say that if Farrah had to choose between her career and Lee, there is absolutely no question that she would decide on Lee. Her trust in him is so profound that Farrah, weaned on Catholicism, even made up her mind to live with him prior to marriage. Clearly the arrangement did not shake her strong religious foundations, for today she still counts rosary beads and keeps little Mass announcements in her car. As a wife she remains totally devoted.

Her marriage is so important that Farrah has told friends: "I would like to save up money and take off. All marriages that last are with people who do not live in Los Angeles."

Thus far, the Farrah Fawcett–Lee Majors union is breaking longevity records in Hollywood. Her commitment to the marriage is evident in every article written about her. And her career has enhanced the partnership; in early 1977 she and Lee formed a joint film production company.

Among the comments Farrah has made on marriage to various publications are the following:

"I dash home, jump in the shower, spray on some perfume, and greet Lee at the door with a cool drink and a kiss. And I still like to cook our dinners."

reflectively . . .

"I've done some growing up in the past six years. Looking back, I was like a pampered little china doll in that big house. My husband would go to work at dawn and come home after dark. He'd call to say there are problems on the set and he'd be late, and I'd tell him: 'You mean, after I cooked you this really terrific dinner, you're gonna let it spoil?' On weekends he'd be dead on his feet and I'd pull at him to take me out. Well, needless to say, all this has changed. Lee and I are in the same boat now."

then . . .

"I try to spend as much time with Lee as possible. We're devoted to each other. He couldn't be happier for me. I'm not sure what the future may bring. Things are great now, but I prefer to live one day at a time."

confessing . . .

"I've never had the burning ambition that a lot of actresses have. But if I ever got to the point of having to choose between marriage and a career, I would say that it would mean my marriage was on the decline anyway."

lovingly . . .

"When you really love somebody, I don't think competition really enters in. Lee is very happy and very proud about what is happening for me, just like I am for him."

analytically . . .

"I'm still going through an adjustment period; it still comes as a surprise when strangers recognize me. And they want to see me look a certain way. Lee, on the other hand, can just jump up, not shave, and he still looks incredible!"

proudly . . .

"Of course I'm totally in love with Lee and wouldn't want any other man in the world, but any woman is bound to appreciate a man's paying attention to her."

firmly . . .

"I know Lee, and I know our relationship."

Career

If the pressure ever became too unbearable, Farrah Fawcett-Majors vows that she would chuck her career. That, obviously, has not happened. At one point, after dropping ten pounds and suffering severe exhaustion, Farrah and her co-Angels were given a three-day hiatus. But they were back on the job immediately thereafter.

Thus far her career is going nowhere but up. Along the way this sweet southern girl has become wise to the ways of Hollywood. Of her childhood she recalls, "I was never rebellious. I never wanted to be that way, I liked being protected, and I always felt that being sheltered gave a girl certain advantages that she wouldn't get if she became too wise too early." Being something of a pragmatist, Farrah figured that it was time to get the necessary exposure. Still she remains unjaded and as optimistic as ever about the future.

Recently Farrah said:

> "Don't get me wrong, I'm no cream puff. Well, I hope not, anyway. I mean, I don't think I let people walk all over me. But then, I usually don't have to worry. You hear so much about Hollywood being a jungle and that everyone who enters it becomes bitter and disillusioned. I've been lucky: almost everyone has been very kind to me. That makes me feel really good."

"It's a funny thing—the audience often builds up its heroes, then can hardly wait to tear them down. But I've always known this is a very fickle business, which is one reason I don't put everything I've got into pursuing a career."

joyfully . . .

"It's very gratifying to give a good perform-ance and you can't say, 'Gee, it's not wonder-ful having that 90 percent of the fans come up and say wonderful things to you.' Forget about the 10 percent who don't! I think any actress who says she doesn't enjoy that is lying to herself—because it is great, and it makes me happy and my parents happy. I get a great deal of satisfaction out of that."

honestly . . .

"My image is one of glamour, and that's what people expect. And I understand that."

openly . . .

"There's more to me than just hair and a smile. I like to think I'm funny and sort of a comedienne. Anyway, I'm not sure I'd like to be cast as a sex symbol. The most important thing, to me, is to enjoy my work and be given the chance to do different things."

jokingly . . .

"The first show I was so scared I could barely say my lines. Now, if I make a mistake

I can joke about it with the crew. I tell them, 'What the hell, gang, it's only me, old screw-up.' "

defiantly . . .

"When I'm feeling pressured I think, 'How dare people keep taking and taking. Must I keep giving and giving?' "

When it comes to money, Farrah believes in her talent and thus can ask for money commensurate with it. Rarely suffering from self-doubt, Farrah knows how to drive a hard bargain. "I'm the only one who knows what I am truly worth," Farrah says, "and at this point in my life I'm not going to compromise."

The money is a by-product of hard work as opposed to an end in itself. Farrah is not motivated to become the wealthiest citizen in Hollywood. Her idea is to buy freedom and privacy with her earnings. Friends report that Farrah often says, "I want to save up and take off." At the age of thirty she even talks about retiring one day. Assuredly, Farrah is not someone who gets caught up in the excitement of making money. Rather it is the notion that with a bulging bank account she will not have to think about money. Instead she will be free to enjoy the fruits of her industry.

Farrah, by all accounts, is not profligate. Her wardrobe is largely furnished by the "Charlie's Angels" budget. What she wears on the show she gets to keep. Coming from a middle class background where her parents wisely saw that there was always enough so that their daughter could have what she wanted, Farrah knows the value of not living beyond her means. Her generosity is mostly directed toward her family, particularly her parents. She does not buy people's affections or try to impress them with lavish parties or gifts. When she does buy someone a present, it is always something tasteful and of good quality.

Colleagues say that Farrah is responsible and honorable about money. If the wardrobe people bring her clothes she does not want to wear, she feels that the correct thing is to return the outfits. She cannot be pressured into giving things away. This includes presents. Once Farrah was reminded that she had forgotten to get someone a gift, and her response was mild annoyance. Simply, this is a girl who likes to act on her own rather than be coerced into doing something that she does not feel at the moment.

"Farrah has a real sense of herself," says Cathy Amsterdam. "She knows what she wants and what's good for her."

Farrah is a curious combination of someone genuinely concerned about others' well-being, but at the same time she does not want to become caught up in their problems. "Farrah is very attentive to people who work with her," says a colleague. "But at the same time she is distant. Lee's distance is blatant. Farrah is more subtle."

The reaction she inspires: "Farrah pushes the buttons in you. She makes you want to protect her. Yet it is hard to get close to someone who remains distant."

As a woman of action rather than of contemplation, Farrah, according to some, has no time for insecurities and does not like to be around people who do not have a good self-image.

Both Farrah and Lee are better able to express their feelings on paper. "They're big on writing notes to each other," a friend says. "Memos left around the house read like love letters."

The ever-cautious Farrah may say that she has had an argument with Lee but will never reveal the details of it. "They're both volatile people," a friend says. "Farrah may throw the phone and Lee will sulk. But a few hours later they are like lovebirds. They were made for each other."

Says her secretary: "Farrah considers what she tells people. Certain things she does not feel that she should reveal to people. And she doesn't."

One motivation may be the way that Farrah views Hollywood: "It is like a big high school where everybody swaps stories. A man I've said hello to a few times is telling people that I've gone to bed with him. Why should I bring myself down to that level?" She refuses to listen to or spread gossip. However, she confesses concern about the effect on her husband and parents: "My parents read those things and ask, 'What about that?' I can't protect myself against that kind of thing."

Farrah clearly resents rumors that the Angels are doing battle with each other. "I've never had a feud with anybody in my life," she says, adding, "It's just too bad when people have to dream up cat fights between female co-stars to drum up excitement."

Though Farrah is on the advisory board of the

Women's Bank of Los Angeles, she does not embrace feminism. "Any woman who says she doesn't use her femininity to get what she wants is deceiving herself," she told *People* magazine. "Men don't have our instinct, and we don't have their strength."

Again, Farrah will trade on her femininity only so far. On several occasions she has refused to do scenes in a bikini. "I told them I refused to be used that way," she says. "I have no objection to wearing a bikini on this show, but not simply because they've reached a quiet point in the script and need my body to liven things up. I won't be used that way."

Of her success as an Angel, Farrah says: "People are ready for glamour on TV. Women like watching women. The chemistry between us works."

Farrah remains unflappable by shrugging off ugly gossip and refusing to ransack her brain for reasons as to why she is the beneficiary of so much success.

Her philosophy is best summed up by this statement about the future from Farrah, who says that personal dreams are "all being taken care of. I believe that if a person is born and they are exceptionally blessed, they have at one time or another paid their dues.

"In my mind this is how I justify sickness, or the fact that one person is born crippled or blind or whatever. In my own mind, it's a way for me to justify my own blessings and not feel guilty. I think I've already probably paid some dues, and I'm extremely grateful for my blessings.

"And I have a feeling that in this life, at this particular time for me, everything's being taken care of for me. God has been very good to me, and I've been very blessed."

Chapter 9

Farrah's Future

The class of '65 at W. B. Ray High School in Corpus Christi, Texas, had its share of striking young women. It was testimony to the belief held by many that Texas breeds many of the most dazzling beauties in the country and the world.

Today that tradition continues at Ray. Young girls, their slender, bronzed arms hugging textbooks, grace the concrete benches, donated by each graduating class, on the front lawn shaded by palm and moss trees.

Some of these golden girls would go on to careers, and others to marriage. One graduate of the class of '65 went on to both in the most spectacular way. She was the fairest of them all. Her name was Farrah Fawcett.

By the time Farrah reached her teenage years, she was already a local phenomenon, the most beautiful girl in the high school. Today, twelve years later, her territory stretches across the length and breadth of the land. Simply, Farrah Fawcett-Majors has captivated much of America.

There seem to be no boundaries to the affection and adoration that she inspires in the public. A poster, showing her in a red bathing suit, has at last count sold more than 2.4 million copies, putting her well ahead of some of the most popular pinups of the past. Her publicist receives hundreds of interview requests daily. As many as 30,000 letters at a time flood the "Charlie's Angels" office—and they're for Farrah!

So far, there is no sign of a let-up. Recently Liz Smith reported in her New York *Daily News* column "The tidal wave that almost swamped *Los Angeles* magazine when they got ready to print their April cover featuring Farrah Fawcett-Majors in a plunging, clingy swim suit has yet to subside." Then she quoted the magazine's president Seth Baker as calling the scene a nightmare: "Her fans shut down the switchboard, blocked our way into the office, and disrupted everything trying to get advance copies. For the first time in our history we had to check identifications. Even the printer was throwing people out. If this keeps up, we're going to have to come up with a new freedom of the press—from Farrah's fans!"

That same month, April, Farrah Fawcett-Majors also decorated the covers of both *Vogue* and *McCalls*. And *New West* already had still another front-page splash in the works.

The New Pin-Up-Girl, as she is known, was billed by leading fashion-magazine *Vogue* as the "New Kind of Cover Girl, New Kind of Beauty." Farrah, who made her reputation as a commercials and TV actress rather than a magazine model, was described further by that publication as the "star of our All-Out Fitness issue—if ever you need convincing that healthy is beautiful, Farrah is it!"

Unquestionably—and recent history has proved this to be the case—looking at Farrah has been good for circulation. Almost every major publication in the country seemed to arrive at the same diagnosis. Even *People* put Farrah smack in the center of its year-end issue cover graced by pictures of, among others, President Jimmy Carter. Newspapers have also pumped out major features on Farrah. Hardly a day passes, too, when there is not at least one small item about her. And the tabloids continue to throb with tales of Farrah's personal life.

The plethora of interview requests has resulted in an almost comical situation, with at least one of Farrah's most trusted agents becoming almost inaccessible to the press. In a major feature, written by Sean Mitchell of the Dallas *Times Herald*, Farrah's commercial agent, Marge Schicktanz, was quoted for about two paragraphs about how difficult it was to book Farrah at first because of her special beauty and also how her client stacks up against magazine models like Margaux Hemingway. Schicktanz's remarks were prefaced by "in a rare interview." Recently Schicktanz told a Los Angeles *Times* fashion writer, doing an article on Farrah's hair, that it was "very rare" for her [Schicktanz] to grant an interview. The interview was conducted by phone, and the writer recalls amusedly, "She keeps you waiting on the line longer than the President."

Like others who work for the superstar, Schicktanz is enormously protective, loyal, and devoted to her client. That closeness has made a Schicktanz interview—almost by osmosis—a so-called journalistic coup. Assuredly, Farrah's publicist Jay Bernstein will have a long shopping list at Christmastime. A genial man, he sends reporters gifts, though such fringe benefits are outlawed in most city rooms. Always, his fertile imagination—that same imagination that has turned Farrah into the media's favorite merchandise—is at work. This creativity is evident in his choice of presents. Jonathan Larsen, once a Los Angeles correspondent for *Time* magazine and now editor of *New Times* magazine, recalls receiving a unique cigarette holder, shaped like a donkey. Bernstein takes calls day and night on behalf of his client.

"Farrah Fawcett-Majors is a media heroine—not a cultural heroine," says Ray Browne, a professor of Popular Culture and English at Bowling Green University in Ohio. "She is both a fad and a heroine. The latter depends on her being very much in the public eye. As long as she remains in the public eye, we like her. Unless we find another person, we'll remember her. But Americans have shown their capacity for finding another."

Her emergence as a heroine, Browne explains, grows out of a "need we have to be somewhat liberated but not dangerously exposed. Farrah represents a longing on our part, a kind of nostalgia, a return to the safe and good old days."

Reflecting on Farrah's designation as America's sex symbol, Browne comments: "Farrah is virginal. She is the very attractive girl next-door rather than the sex goddess down the street at the movie house. She does not represent sex except in the safest sense of the word. She is too young to be sexy. Both Farrah and Angie Dickinson ('Policewoman') play similar roles, but they are worlds apart. Angie is womankind, sultry, sexy. Farrah is the young girl whom you look at and don't touch and *strikingly* don't *want* to touch."

Browne attempts to prove his point with a shaving cream commercial in which Farrah sits in a man's hand. "She wiggles her behind over his hand in every conceivable way, but she does not compromise her position in the spot. Although she has all the motions of a seductress, you could show the commercial in a Sunday school."

"Charlie's Angels" is, in Browne's view, "a kind of trinity of liberated women who pretty much do what they want. They're pure and virginal after every episode. They are liberated, but safe. Probably the best illustration of this spirit is Farrah's hair. It is free, but not windblown. Her hair suggests a kind of controlled freedom."

On the wall of his Popular Culture classroom there is a Farrah Fawcett-Majors poster. "I was playing around and put paper over Farrah from her neck down," Browne recalls. "Then I touched her bosom and said to my students, 'Excuse me!' Only two students snickered. The point was that Farrah's charm is from the shoulders up." He adds, "Behind Farrah is a Navajo blanket, and this makes her a free spirit."

The professor concedes that his opinion may not be shared by others. After being quoted in a newspaper about Farrah's above-the-shoulders sex appeal, Browne says he received a letter from an angry California man who argued, simply, "It's her nipples!" Farrah jokes that she is popular because she sometimes doesn't wear a bra on "Charlie's Angels." This, of course, depends on what outfit she is wearing on the segment.

Other observers claim that our perception of what is sexy has changed radically in the last few years. And Farrah is symbolic of this new sexuality. Many younger men, they say, prefer females who are built more like little boys than top-heavy middle-aged women. Pre-teenage boys, who are among Farrah's most ardent fans, can better identify with a woman who stirs up fantasies but does not thrust reality on them. Traditionally, tomboys have been the most popular girls in grade school. Young boys are often bewitched by women who can throw a football or play catch with a hardball. Adventure is in the air.

Dr. Alan Rosenberg, a New York psychiatrist, told the *National Enquirer* that "innocence and bold abandon are the wildest combination sexually to a man. These two factors, which Farrah has, are enough to make America go bananas."

In one of the most perceptive analyses of the Farrah Fawcett-Majors phenomenon, Roger Rosenblatt wrote in *The New Republic*: "Farrah has teeth and a bottom, and her celebrated hair looks like a cartoon of hair, which is appropriate for comedy. But her most appealing comic attribute is that she takes it easy on us, playing the opposite of a *belle dame sans merci*, not a Carmen or a Salammbo, not the European Fatal Woman to lead us through romantic agony, but as *Time* describes her, 'a warm, giggly sort of girl,' who implies, as Mae West used to hum aloud, 'Come on, boys: sex won't kill you.' It's an assurance that we cannot hear too often."

"What constitutes sexuality in an age of sexual freedom? The same thing it always did, only more so. The greater the freedom, the greater the fear. The greater the fear, the louder the laugh. So here's Farrah, not witty like Lombard, not humorous like West or Monroe, but just as funny in her fashion. She doesn't crack jokes: she is one—sitting pretty at poolside, tossing back her celestial curls, and flashing those choppers at millions of boys who, as ever, will wink, hoot, whistle, and elbow each other in the ribs, but will *never* come up to see her sometime."

Among the few journalists who have not been bitten by the FF-M mystique is Chicago *Daily News* syndicated columnist Mike Royko who claims: "Every time I see a picture of Farrah Fawcett-Majors, the nation's sex symbol, nothing happens. I don't have any unspeakable thoughts, or pant, or say boy-oh-boy-oh-boy, or otherwise express my admiration. The first time nothing happened, I thought it might be the cold weather. The next time, I got a little worried. The third time I conducted a test on myself. I looked up some pictures of Sophia Loren, Marilyn Monroe, and Raquel Welch. Within moments I had at least six unspeakable thoughts . . ."

Talking about past national sex symbols, Royko says, "Rita Hayworth, for example, was almost always shown wearing a loosely clinging negligee while sprawling cat-like on a large bed. The bed appeared too soft for proper support, which could lead to a backache, but that seemed irrelevant. Whenever I saw Miss Hayworth's pictures, I knew what she had in mind. Or at least I knew what she

133

had in mind for me to have in my mind. Because that was what I immediately had in mind.

"But the last time I saw Ms. Fawcett-Majors she was on TV doing a commercial for a health club. She was all over the screen, straining at one machine, kicking another, tugging, bending, and working up a heck of a sweat. So I'm not sure what Ms. Fawcett-Majors has in mind. Whatever it is, a man might develop a hernia before he got around to it."

Nonetheless, tens of thousands of people have grabbed on to this sex symbol. The poster of Farrah, for $2.50 apiece, is expected to sell 10 million copies. Other sex symbols did not kick in such big sales. Raquel Welch's poster has sold two million copies; Marilyn Monroe, 1.5; and Lindsay Wagner has sold 500,000 copies. A poster of Lee Majors, the Six-Million-Dollar Man and the husband of Farrah, has sold 500,000.

Farrah's mane alone has created a mania. Hairstylists in every city in the country say that hordes of women are flocking to their shops for the Farrah Fawcett-Majors cut. Asked why they want that look, many of them reply: "My husband (or boyfriend) wants me to look like Farrah Fawcett." At the May Company, a medium to-low-priced Los Angeles department store, Angel wigs are on sale for $35 in their millinery department. "Ask for Angel Girl," their ads say.

In Linwood, Kansas, a town of 354 on the western fringe of Kansas City, the fad flared to a dangerous point. On Valentine's Day, a fourteen-year-old cheerleader was attacked, apparently by jealous classmates, after she did her hair in the style worn by Farrah. As the eighth-grader opened her locker, another girl poured nitric acid on her from behind.

"The plan was to damage her hair to the point where she would have to get it cut," school principal Bill Chambers told the Associated Press. "The hairdo was mentioned prominently in statements given to juvenile authorities by all seven girls involved in the incident." One girl carried out the attack, and six others talked about it with the perpetrator or knew it was coming. All of them were suspended from school.

The attack left the girl, who lives with her parents on a 320-acre farm a few miles east of Linwood, with burns on her back and shoulder. She also had to restyle her singed hair. "We just thank God every day that she didn't turn her head when this happened," her mother said. Two of the girls had been in school with her daughters since kindergarten and according to her father, "They come from fine families—they take their children to church and 4-H."

Ironically, Farrah's appeal is to the wholesome, wide open space spirit of the heartland of America, in places like Linwood, Kansas. But she has such fierce fans that sometimes they cannot contain their feelings. For this reason, Farrah the Free Spirit can no longer move about as easily as she did before becoming one of "Charlie's Angels."

Some of her commercials are aimed at the sporty crowd. In a television commercial introducing the 1977 line of Mercury-Cougar automobiles, the scene is a stretch of California beach. The time is midnight; a lone figure emerges from the water. She walks up the beach, pauses, and starts to unzip a wetsuit. As the suit comes off, a gorgeous blonde is revealed, now wearing an evening gown. She walks to a waiting car where her co-star will be a real live cougar. Of course an animal trainer is hidden and holding the cat in place. Once again, Farrah Fawcett-Majors is involved in a scene, this time a commercial, with inherent danger and a wild animal lurking in her presence. Yet the mood is tame, almost peaceful.

Farrah's every movement or word creates a commotion. Recently there has been talk of her not returning to "Charlie's Angels" for the next season, and of her husband Lee Majors also bowing out of his TV series, "The Six-Million-Dollar Man." The couple themselves announced that they would not be back. They have a production company called Fawcett-Majors Productions, and both of them appear to want to move out of television and into movies.

Some TV critics interpret the move as a ploy to pry more money out of the ABC network. Right now, Farrah earns $5,000 per segment from Spelling-Goldberg Productions, which makes "Charlie's Angels." Reportedly the fee was going up to $10,000 next season. When more money is involved, generally it is up to the network, unhappy about losing a superstar of a top-rated series, to ante up the extra money.

At issue is a claim by Farrah that she does not have a contract for next season's "Angels" because she never signed an agreement. However the Spelling-Goldberg people offer a different view. Says Brett Garwood, executive coordinator of Spelling-Goldberg: "The contract was never signed on Farrah's end. But our interpretation is that there is still a contract since she performed and received a salary while working for 'Charlie's Angels.'" The contract is binding, they say, because it includes an option clause for '77-78. Already Spelling-Goldberg attorney Bill Hayes has filed a lawsuit against her for breach of contract.

Garwood continues: "I have known Farrah for eight years, and I love her, and I am fond of her. I do think she has a rare commodity, a certain magic, that is unusual. The sale of her poster is proof of this."

But the show must go on, and in television, business is business—and it's tough. Should Farrah decide not to return and lose the lawsuit, she could be faced with suspension from the industry for as long as two years. This would mean that she would be enjoined from working on any other projects.

Striking an ominous note, Garwood points out that a two-year suspension could have less than a salutary effect. "Others who have not honored their contracts have tended to drop out of sight very quickly. Martin Landau and Barbara Bain who were on 'Mission Impossible' are two examples that come to mind." Their careers went into an eclipse, except for appearances outside the country; the two are now on "Space 1999," science fiction show with relatively low ratings.

A producer in the industry warns that an outfit like Spelling-Goldberg is a giant in the field and thus has King Kong-like power to crush a performer whom they believed reneged on a contract. "One has to understand that breaking a contract with people as powerful as Spelling-Goldberg could have disastrous ripples throughout the entire industry," he says. "At the same time, I'd hitch myself to Farrah's star in a second. I think she is going all the way to the top, and I would like to be along for the ride."

Joseph Finnegan in the "Hollywood Report" for *TV Guide* offers this opinion on Farrah's declaration that she would not return for an Angel: "It is spring, the time of year when one can confidently expect some top series performers to announce they won't be back. It's a tradition almost as old as television itself. Lucille Ball did it for years, holding out until CBS met her annual demands. Peter Falk picked up the ploy when Lucy retired. And now we have Farrah Fawcett-Majors ... Farrah, who has suddenly become America's No. 1 sex symbol, is in a bargaining position almost unprecedented for a TV personality."

His conclusion: "Close observers predict that concessions will be made, salaries will be raised, and the couple will be back. The frosting on the cake will be a theatrical movie costarring Lee and Farrah. Such a deal would give both of them a shot at the movie careers they seek."

If this be the case, Farrah would make *Foul Play* for Paramount. The director would be Colin Higgins, author of *Silver Streak*.

Yet back in March, Farrah phoned her friend Shanny Lott, sister of her college sweetheart, in Austin and vowed: "If they offer me a million dollars I am not going to do 'Charlie's Angels.' I want to be an actress in the movies."

Observers of the Farrah Fawcett-Majors phenomenon say that her posture grows out of a feeling on Farrah's part that her fame is fleeting, that she should cash in on her celebrity status before all the resources dry up. But other people, many of whom have worked with Farrah, insist that she is here to stay. She has a magical quality, they say, and this will continue to entice the public for a long time to come. "Farrah is no flash-in-the-pan," they say repeatedly.

Whatever Farrah decides, the controversy created by her announcement has kept her in the public eye. *Newsday* TV critic syndicated columnist Marvin Kitman says: "I would be surprised if Farrah dropped out of the show. It would be self-destructive. It's a self-promotion thing to stay on the show. Constant exposure makes anything a cult, a phenomenon, and you cannot discount this."

Kitman, probably the most irreverent TV critic in the country and certainly the most wonderfully wry, is currently working on what he bills as a "scholarly paper. It's about How Many Angels Can Dance on the Head of a Pin. Three or thirty or two—if Farrah doesn't return. It opens up a lot of possibilities. This is very bewildering."

Though he sounds as witty and wildly absurd as humor columnist Art Buchwald, TV critic Kitman claims, "I'm much better-looking." Unabashedly and amusedly, Kitman confesses that he is the last critic in America to study the Farrah Fawcett-Majors phenemenon: "I haven't reviewed the program yet. I hope she's fooling around about the threat to leave."

While Kitman explains that Farrah's flawless appearance fills a need in people who do not want to be confronted with reality, he has reservations about her role as a detective. "I don't think it is practical for Farrah to have hair like that. If she fired a gun, it could get caught in it. It may be a bad thing for girls who want to be private eyes.

They think they have to have long hair—and that will be their undoing."

Should Farrah give up crime-fighting she may be flicking her hair back in a romantic novel, *Sweet Savage Love*, by bestselling author Rosemary Rogers. Currently Lee Majors and the author are in negotiations to buy movie rights to the book. The parties are expected to sign a deal by May, with the shooting to start in June. Unlike the Paramount picture, the couple would own the property.

A script has already been written for the film. The producer has also been picked. He is Roy Higgins, who made the successful "Captains and the Kings" TV Series. Farrah would play Virginia Brandon, who falls in love with Steve Morgan, with Lee Majors, of course, in that role. It is an exotic love story with the heroine moving through England, France, Mexico, and to the southwest United States, Farrah's home turf, in Texas and Arizona.

Says author Rosemary Rogers: "Farrah is the most perfect person in the world for the part of Virginia Brandon. Her looks are the greatest and her spirit seems appropriate for the part. Virginia Brandon is beautiful, but strong-willed and with a touch of nonworldly innocence."

"Anybody has a right to do what they dream," says psychologist Dr. Joyce Brothers. "Farrah's dream is to be a movie star." Then she speculates: "She'll probably do both 'Charlie's Angels' and movies. They'll make time."

Describing Farrah as "very warm and very charming," Dr. Joyce Brothers says that this superstar has a quality whereby "everything is a surprise and a delight to her rather than an attitude of I've got it coming to me."

They met at the ABC Battle of the Network Stars where Dr. Brothers was giving some psychological commentary on the competitors. "Farrah has an innocence not in terms of being unaware, but in the sense that she is not manipulative."

At their meeting Farrah told Dr. Brothers that she would like to go on a talk show with her. "Her reason was that she thinks I'll make her look good," Dr. Brothers recalls. "It fascinated me that anyone that beautiful needed any kind of support. I don't believe this girl knows how vulnerable she is."

She continues: "No one since Marilyn Monroe has caused such a furor. I first met Marilyn when she was an unknown model, at a charity benefit. Even then I sensed she was going to go straight up. You rarely see that kind of excitement. That same thing will happen to Farrah. But I have a feeling this girl can be hurt."

During the Battle of the Network Stars, Farrah rooted so hard for her ABC teammates that she lost her voice and missed a full two days of work. But, as always, Farrah was on the winning side and walked off with $20,000, awarded to each member of the ABC team, in prize money.

Farrah, who added points to the team's tally, showed her drive and energy in a bicycle rally. The competitive fire she brings to athletic feats is evident in almost every other area of her life. Ever since Farrah was a little girl, she always tried her best and usually came out on top.

Should Farrah become a movie actress, friends say, she would work hard and succeed at it. Both a producer and a director of "Charlie's Angels" say that Farrah has the makings of a first-rate comedienne.

To date, her track record has been practically perfect. Always on time and then giving every endeavor her all, Farrah has gone a long distance. Each stride has been forward-moving and a vertical progression. The next move, though, may be the most crucial.

Many people in the entertainment field feel that if Farrah were to continue on "Charlie's Angels" for at least another season, this would allow her more experience and also a good showcase. It would be a base from which to operate effectively in other spheres, such as motion pictures.

Timing seems to be a major factor. These same people think that Farrah may not be ready for a quantum leap into cinema. This, of course, would depend on what type of part she is given to play in a movie. "Farrah would never take lessons," says a friend. "She just isn't the type."

Thus "Charlie's Angels" could be her training ground. Director Allen Baron, who worked on one of the early segments and then one of the last, says that he saw progress on Farrah's part in that short time. Others concur in this opinion. There is talk, too, that the scripts may be upgraded to create a broader range of acting for the Angels and this conceivably could be a drawing card to retain Farrah.

Whatever the outcome, the eyes of not only Texas but also the rest of the country will be upon her. Every word out her gleaming mouth becomes instant headlines. Whether or not Farrah continues as an Angel has become a favorite guessing game with an element of mystery to it.

That such attention continues unabated is a source of wonderment to the star herself. The fact that Farrah has never made a public fuss about herself may, in part, be the cause of all this attention. Usually it is people who are comfortable with themselves and content who attract others. Desperate characters, of which Farrah has never been one, tend to repel people. Farrah herself does not like to be around downbeat personalities. There is too much to celebrate in life, hers included!

Even in these trying times, when Farrah's future is uncertain and somewhat topsy-turvy, she appears to be in complete control of her destiny. Despite the pull of people around her—she seems to collect one more each day—in the end it will be Farrah who makes up her own mind.

Knowing and making up her own mind has been a characteristic of Farrah ever since she was a child growing up in Corpus Christi. Neighbors and teachers applauded her strong, well-defined character. What Farrah showed the public just skimmed the surface. Always, on the basis of her actions, they knew there was more than met the eye. And what met the eye, even during childhood was, a breathtaking sight. "Farrah looked just like an angel," Corpus Christi citizens often say.

As a seventh-grader at parochial school, a nun remembers, Farrah was somewhat detached from the rest of the girls. "I never figured out what happened," she says, "but Farrah sort of pulled back. Something was bothering her. I don't know whether it was that some of the girls were jealous. Yet it did not interfere with Farrah's performance.

She did not let any troubles get in the way of her homework."

Karen Spellings, who attended parochial school with Farrah and later caught up with her at the University of Texas, remembers how she would try to make Farrah a conspirator in the lipstick caper: "Right before Mass I would tell Farrah to come into the bathroom. We'd put on lipstick. As soon as the nuns would see us, we would be marched right to the principal's office. Farrah didn't want to do it that often. I think that was the only bad thing she ever did in school."

In high school Farrah earned the same high marks from teachers and classmates. She did not forge her way into various school activities. In fact, there is no record of her having participated in any clubs or groups. Yet everybody knew Farrah Fawcett. She was the class beauty who did not flaunt her looks. At the same time, she did not judge others by their physical appearance or put much stock in popularity. Once Farrah made up her mind that she liked someone that was it. She was not one to rely on what everybody else thought of that person. Friends were friends, and Farrah treasured them.

At the University of Texas at Austin Farrah was a trendsetter among traditionalists. While everybody paraded around in prim outfits, Farrah favored a more casual style befitting an artist. Though Farrah pledged a sorority, she perceived the potential boredom inherent in this system. More than this, Farrah has never been a person who could be stratified, straitjacketed, into a societal role. She has always been her own person. She is neither a leader nor a follower. Farrah just obeys her own instincts and somehow achieves a balance within herself and with the world at large.

Her arrival in Hollywood was still another symbol of her individualism. Her mother drove her there. Once on her own, she was never swayed by the values of the community. Farrah would never compromise herself. She wanted to be sure that she had gotten ahead on her own. And she was quite sure that success was possible for her. She worked hard and was serious about her professional future. But she also was not consumed by a drive that would cancel out the fun and newness of the experience. Fear of the unknown did not prevent Farrah from getting the most out of these years. She has always known her worth and was not about to cheat herself out of the promise of a good life there.

Once again, her specialness surfaced on the show. Though her co-stars are also beautiful, it was Farrah who emerged from the start as the superstar. Some people say that Jaclyn Smith is prettier than Farrah and that Kate Jackson is certainly the most intellectually gifted and experienced as an actress, Farrah became the Golden Mean. In America she came to reflect the good life, the ideal.

More than a year has passed since Farrah skyrocketed to success. Beneath the gilded exterior there is as yet no tarnishing. Though the Angels play fairly predictable parts, which match their lines, Farrah has not grown rusty in her role. She just gets better all the time.

Beneath the seeming flash of Farrah, there is a durable quality. Otherwise she would not be so revered by the public. In the past there have been cults that have grown up around a character and then vanished just as fast as they got started. For a time everybody was captivated by Davy Crockett. People bought the trademark fur hat and made trips to the Alamo. The clamor was about the character, not the actor playing the part.

In a matter of weeks she met the man with whom she would make a life. It was love-at-first-sight. This may have been her luckiest break, and today she still cherishes her husband, Lee Majors. He was a kind of buffer for Farrah against the hardness of Hollywood. If Farrah had plotted the scenario, she could not have come up with a more ideal mate. Farrah is not a schemer. If anything, it is her natural, unaffected approach to living that opens her up, almost unconsciously, to good experiences.

Meanwhile she was working hard at whatever commercials came her way and devoting the rest of the time to a stable marriage and home life. After guesting on Lee's show a few times and getting small parts in shows like "I Dream of Jeannie," Farrah moved into movies. Perhaps her worst experience was the first film *Myra Breckinridge*, but she did not dwell on her disappointment. The fault lay with the movie, not with Farrah. In a later film, *Logan's Run*, Farrah would repair the damage with a respectable performance. Finally, there was "Charlie's Angels," which catapulted Farrah to superstardom in a matter of months.

The national fascination is with Farrah, not Kelly the Angel. The public is not racing out to get Angel outfits. They are searching out Farrah Fawcett-Majors—her hair, her figure, her style.

They are not even reenacting scenes from the show as people who grew up with walkie-talkies did with "Captain Video." Farrah is no gimmick, game, toy. She is a person—the person many people would like to become or at least look like.

What may be her undoing is that people are not waiting and watching for Farrah to slip into a role. She *is* the fantasy in the flesh. This is the way they want to view her. So whether or not Farrah stays with "Charlie's Angels" or devotes herself solely to motion pictures, will not make much difference in the public's vision of her.

The curiosity is that her most ardent fans do not want to see Farrah change one thing about herself. Her smile is romance for them. So are her alive leaf-green eyes. Farrah's part is cut out for her—she is Farrah to her fans. Another identity, even in a two-hour movie, won't enhance or hurt her popularity.

Fans ask nothing more of Farrah than that they get to look at her. While her current posture may satisfy them, it does not serve Farrah's needs. She is a person who has grown at every stage of her life, and she wants to continue doing so. A stationary position, immortalized by a poster, is not sufficient for a woman who believes that she can become a top movie actress. She is someone who will not set limitations on herself because this stifles and paralyzes a person. Like her hair, Farrah moves.

"People want to see me in a certain way," she told *Coronet* magazine. "I understand this. Still, I think deep down every actress would like to do a role where she doesn't wear any makeup, where she is accepted on her acting alone."

Of her ability Farrah comments: "I don't delude myself about my acting talent. I know I'm not great. I wasn't blessed with that kind of ability, but I think I'm getting better. I think there's hope for me as an actress."

Describing herself as a "basically shy" person, Farrah is vaguely embarrassed by the flurry of excitement about her. Essentially it is a matter of not understanding exactly why she is today the No. 1 sex symbol in America and worshipped at every turn by an adoring public. Her bafflement is not an act! It is real, just as are her other responses, and this seems to charm people even more.

Part of the intrigue is that no one can pinpoint what touched the romantic nerve of Americans. With a great talent like Barbra Streisand, fans can be precise about her appeal. A great singer. A splendid actress. And now an Academy Award-winning composer, as well as a producer. Farrah on the other hand, is like a floating object, drifting in and rarely out of the national psyche day in and day out.

How long Farrah will be lodged in the hearts and minds of the people is a question that no one can answer. At best, the guess is for as long as she chooses to grace the screen—whether as an Angel or as Virginia Brandon or both.

Some cynics say that if Farrah were to make the transition now to a major motion picture role, she might flop. Clearly tens of thousands of fans would rush to her rescue. During the Ford for President campaign, Farrah, as one of the celebrities appearing on his behalf, was mobbed by the public at every stop. Secret Service men offered her protection.

That is, after they took a few seconds out to pose with her for a picture at a private party for Ford given by Sammy Davis, Jr., and his wife. "I've never seen anything like this before," Ray Caldiero, head of the entertainment troops for the campaign and a Marriott Hotel vice-president, recalls. "Have you ever seen Secret Service men excusing themselves to be photographed with someone? Then they wanted her autograph."

Her victories thus far have proven Farrah to be a winner. But no matter what happens, Farrah will still not suffer defeat. The center of her life is her husband and family, and they will always be there for her. Anything else is just an extra. Disciplined and dedicated, Farrah is not someone who wastes her time on inflated dreams or delusions.

Farrah Fawcett-Majors has come this far, all the way to superstardom, and most probably she will continue by choice on this path. Ever motivated by a desire to do her best, Farrah will assuredly see all her possibilities through.

Yet the trail will never lead Farrah too far from her origins. Along the way, even in the most difficult of times, it is comforting to know that you can go home again. In a sense, Farrah never left. In fact letters to Farrah from fans have ended up in the "Action Line" post office box of the Corpus Christi *Times*. Two letters, according to columnist Lynn Pentony, came from places as far away as Cardiff, South Wales, and Yorkshire, England.

Farrah carries her happy childhood in Corpus Christi to Hollywood. Today she still speaks to that sweetness and joy which fills the soul and mind of America with *speakable* proud thoughts.

Says Farrah Fawcett-Majors: "I never felt I needed to be a star. I always got along in life just fine, which I think has been to my advantage. Because now that it all seems to be happening, I think I might be better equipped to cope with it." She adds that she would like one day to star in a Western.

Chapter 10

Farrah-Fitness

"Good grooming should be a part of everyone's schedule," says Farrah Fawcett-Majors, "because it not only shows you care about and respect yourself, but it makes you more pleasant to be around."

Part of good grooming, she says, is staying in shape. Farrah puts herself through a rigorous daily routine that includes a full calisthenics program and sixty pushups a day. In a *Vogue* article, she told writer Blair Sobol: "Show business has nothing to do with my physical life-style. To me, today's woman has no choice but to get active. I made exercise a part of my life, like brushing my teeth, so I always assume most people are involved with some sort of body movement just to remain alive and survive in this world. Perhaps my physical workouts are my way of getting centered—of getting a grip on myself."

Once a junk food aficionado who liked Cheetos, candy bars, and pecan pies, Farrah was getting emotional hypoglycemic highs and lows, so she switched to protein in small amounts. "I'm not a health-food nut," she continued. "I just listen to my body and follow its instructions—which does call for an occasional Cheetos."

Vogue printed what they called "Farrah's Fresher-Upper":

Brew up a pitcher of Pink Lemon Tea (packaged in bags by Select Tea Co.). Add 12 slices of green apple, sweeten to taste with artificial sweetener. Pour over ice into a tall glass.

The hard part of Farrah's good grooming tips is her hair. All over the country, women are showing up at beauty salons and expecting some minor miracle when they walk out with their Farrah Fawcett-Majors hairstyles. Farrah explains that her hair naturally grows full and abundant. Though she may let it dry naturally a day on the beach, the rest of the time Farrah must work at her hair. When she is working, Hugh York says, Farrah sometimes sleeps in hair rollers. York, who first gave Farrah the famous hairstyle, emphasizes that keeping that style requires a workout too.

On the East Coast, Carl Marraccino, of Marraccino Hair Design in New York's posh East Fifties, agrees with Hugh York. "To keep up the Farrah Fawcett-Majors look," he claims, "girls would need a round-the-clock hairdresser. They can get the look and two hours later it won't be there."

Marraccino, who has set Elizabeth Taylor's hair and cut Barry Newman's, among other celebrities, estimates that one out of twenty girls can wear the

Farrah Fawcett-Majors look. "This means that the hairstyle may stay for two or three days."

As for the cut, Marraccino says that the back can have a V-shape and the front must be cut in layers. "That gives it the bouncy look," he explains. "The cut takes about forty minutes to do."

The Farrah Fawcett-Majors look requires a certain type of hair. "The hair must have a certain amount of body wave to hold the set. A girl needs the best wavy hair—not curly or kinky—and of medium texture. That way it can move in any direction that you want it to go. Hair that is too curly or straight will only go in one direction."

Marraccino follows Hugh York's line of thinking about the Farrah Fawcett-Majors hairstyle: "That look is movement. One length would not fit her personality. She is on the go, on the move. So is her hair."

Nonetheless, Marraccino's artist, Tony Mortellaro, who sketches clients and possible hairstyles to match their looks and personalities, offers a detailed diagram on subsequent pages of how to set and comb out the Farrah Fawcett-Majors hairstyle.

The same individualism that Hugh York brings to clients like Farrah is reflected in the Marraccino approach to hairstyling. In what is known as the Snap-Pic-Cut Method, the artist takes a Polaroid photo, which he translates into a sketch. Then the hair designer analyzes the client's hair and talks to her about her life-style. While her hair is being washed, the artist and the hair designer sketch a batch of new hairstyles for her on transparent overlays. The client checks out the overlays on the sketch of her face and then makes her decision. Only then is her hair cut.

The important thing to keep in mind is that the look fits Farrah Fawcett-Majors, but it may not be for you. Hair is a very individual matter. So much so that Hugh York says, "If I hadn't created that look, Farrah would have." That cascading mane *is* Farrah!

Be yourself—isn't that what Farrah is about? But go ahead, try it.

THE FARRAH FAWCETT-MAJORS LOOK

THE CUT

Farrah Fawcett's famous look starts with a layered haircut on long hair. Starting at the top and holding hair straight up, cut to the desired length (about 3 inches). Using this length as a guide, pull each section of hair straight up, measure to the cut strands and snip off. Hair is almost at a 90-degree angle when cut.

THE SET

Set section of hair across the top in three big pincurls (or vary the style by using rollers).

The crown, back, and nape area rollers are all going down.

Use the large 1½-inch size rollers and set the sides going backwards.

THE COMB-OUT

Take out the rollers and pincurls. Relax the setting pattern by brushing the hair into the desired lines. The top section is very lightly teased and smoothed into soft waves. The hair on the sides and in the back is lightly teased close to the scalp to obtain a firm foundation. The ends are left free to form airy, bouncy waves and curls. After the comb-out, the hair, by going in different directions, shows movement.

Cinchers

Arm stretches

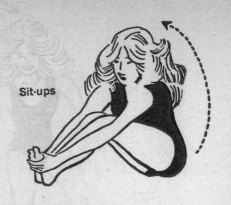

Sit-ups

Thig shapers

Jumping rope

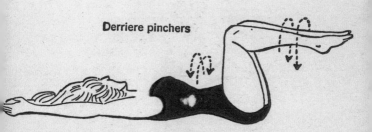

Derriere pinchers

SKETCHES COURTESY OF TONY MORTELLARO

About the Author

Patricia Burstein is a *People* magazine writer who lives and works in New York.

D

Big Bestsellers from SIGNET

☐ **LYNDON JOHNSON AND THE AMERICAN DREAM** by Doris Kearns. (#E7609—$2.50)

☐ **THIS IS THE HOUSE** by Deborah Hill. (#J7610—$1.95)

☐ **LORD RIVINGTON'S LADY** by Eileen Jackson. (#W7612—$1.50)

☐ **ROGUE'S MISTRESS** by Constance Gluyas. (#J7533—$1.95)

☐ **SAVAGE EDEN** by Constance Gluyas. (#J7171—$1.95)

☐ **LOVE SONG** by Adam Kennedy. (#E7535—$1.75)

☐ **THE DREAM'S ON ME** by Dotson Rader. (#E7536—$1.75)

☐ **SINATRA** by Earl Wilson. (#E7487—$2.25)

☐ **SUMMER STATION** by Maud Lang. (#E7489—$1.75)

☐ **THE WATSONS** by Jane Austen and John Coates. (#J7522—$1.95)

☐ **SANDITON** by Jane Austen and Another Lady. (#J6945—$1.95)

☐ **THE FIRES OF GLENLOCHY** by Constance Heaven. (#E7452—$1.75)

☐ **A PLACE OF STONES** by Constance Heaven. (#W7046—$1.50)

☐ **THE ROCKEFELLERS** by Peter Collier and David Horowitz. (#E7451—$2.75)

☐ **THE HAZARDS OF BEING MALE** by Herb Goldberg. (#E7359—$1.75)